THE EXECUTIVE JOB SEARCH

THE EXECUTIVE JOB SEARCH

A Comprehensive Handbook for Seasoned Professionals

ORRIN WOOD

MCGRAW-HILL

NEW YORK   CHICAGO   SAN FRANCISCO   LISBON   LONDON
MADRID   MEXICO CITY   MILAN   NEW DELHI   SAN JUAN
SEOUL   SINGAPORE   SYDNEY   TORONTO

The **McGraw·Hill** *Companies*

Library of Congress Cataloging-in-Publication Data
Wood, Orrin G.
 The executive job search / by Orrin Wood.
  p. cm
 ISBN 0-07-140942-4 (alk. paper)
 1. Career changes—United States. 2. Executives—United States.
3. Job hunting—United States. I. Title.
HF5384.W66 2003
650.14—dc21

                             2003000687

1 2 3 4 5 6 7 8 9 0   DOC/DOC   0 9 8 7 6 5 4 3

ISBN: 0-07-140942-4

This publication is designed to provide accurate and authoritative information in regard to the subject
matter covered. It is sold with the understanding that the publisher is not engaged in rendering legal,
accounting, or other professional service. If legal advice or other expert assistance is required, the
services of a competent professional person should be sought.
                    —From a declaration of principles jointly adopted by a committee of the
                              American Bar Association and a committee of publishers.

This book is printed on recycled, acid-free paper containing a minimum of 50% recycled
de-inked fiber.

McGraw-Hill books are available at special quantity discounts to use as premiums and sales promotions, or for use in corporate training programs. For more information, please write to the Director
of Special Sales, Professional Publishing, McGraw-Hill, Two Penn Plaza, New York, NY 10121-2298.
Or contact your local bookstore.

To my wife, Joan, and my children,
Patsy, Susie, Ned, and Tim, and their families,
who have enriched my life in so many ways

CONTENTS

Preface • xi
How to Find What You're Looking For   xii

Acknowledgments • xiii

1. GETTING PERSPECTIVE • 1
You've Got a Wonderful Opportunity   1
Coping with Losing Your Job   2
You've Got a Lot Going for You   4
Getting Things in Focus   5
How Much of a Factor Is Your Age?   8
Dealing with a Rapidly Changing World   10
Getting What's Yours   11

2. GETING OFF TO A GOOD START • 13
Why a Good Start Is Important   13
Improving Your Mental Outlook   14
Avoiding Pitfalls   14
Dealing with Your Family   17
Good Counseling Can Be a Great Help   18
Organize to Work Efficiently   19
Record Keeping   20

3. DETERMINING YOUR JOB GOALS • 21
Career Phases   21
The Search Process   23
Job Goals   24
Job Priorities   25
Alternative Career Analysis   35
Alternative Job Analysis   41

4. THE JOB SEARCH FROM THE EMPLOYER'S SIDE OF THE DESK • 45
Acknowledging the Employers' Problems   45
Understanding the Difficulties in Recruiting   47

5. IMPROVING YOUR ATTRACTIVENESS TO EMPLOYERS • 55

Presenting Yourself Favorably   55
Remembering All Your Accomplishments   56
Recognizing Your Major Accomplishments   57
Presenting Your Accomplishments   60

6. MAKING YOUR RESUME AN EFFECTIVE TOOL • 67

Perspective   67
Types of Resumes   68
Features of Resumes   69
Tips on Writing Resumes   80
Preparing Your Resume   80
Getting Your Resume Effectively Criticized   81
Some Additional Thoughts on Resume Tips   82
Major Resume Problems   84

7. NETWORKING • 87

How Are You Likely to Get Your Job?   87
Enlarging Your List of Contacts   90
Getting Interviews with Contacts   95
Preparing for Networking Interviews   99
Building Rapport in Networking Interviews   100
Being Alert to Hidden Job Possibilities   101
Getting Good Referrals   102
Getting Good Information on Referrals   103
Getting Personally Introduced to Referrals   103
Giving Something Back in Return   104
Getting More Candid Criticism   105
Developing a Continuing Relationship   106
Analyzing Interview Results and Follow-up   108
Conducting Telephone Interviews When Referrals
   Won't See You   108

8. BLIND PROSPECTING • 111

Overview   111
Target Letter Mailings   113
Telephone Prospecting   113
Broadcast Letter   116
Preparation for Blind Prospecting   118
Record Keeping   119

9. THE VISIBLE MARKET • 121
Executive Recruiters 122
The Internet 123
Answering Ads 124
Job Fairs 127
College Placement Offices 128
Secondary Recruiters 129
When You're Contacted for an Interview 129

10. "JOB HUNTING IS SELLING YOURSELF" • 131
Selling Yourself Is a Key 131
Focus on Improving Your Selling Skills 131
Some Selling Techniques 135
Dealing with Rejection 139

11. PREPARING FOR INTERVIEWS • 141
Researching the Company 142
Research on the Interviewer 143
Your References 144
Being Ready for Tough Questions 145
Practicing Listening and Interviewing 148
Learning from Interviews 148

12. IMPROVING YOUR INTERVIEW EFFECTIVENESS • 149
Perspective 149
The Interview 150
Postinterview Activities 157
Interview Tips 160

13. CONDUCTING AN EFFECTIVE SEARCH • 163
Getting Started 163
Personal Habits 168
Improving Your Productivity 169
Getting Help 174
Checklist for a Dragging Campaign 175

14. EVALUATING OFFERS AND MAKING THE FINAL DECISION • 183
The Process 183
Stalling Offers 184
Getting More Information on the Job and Company 185
Using an Offer to Get Others 186
Negotiating Compensation 187

    Evaluating Offers   190
    After the Final Decision   191

15. SHOULD YOU MAKE A JOB CHANGE? (IF YOU HAVE A CHOICE) • 195

    Myths About Changing Jobs   196
    Why Are You Frustrated?   197
    Your Improvement Program   198
    Get Another Job in the Company   206
    How to Leave Your Company   207
    When an Executive Recruiter Knocks on the Door   209

16. ALTERNATIVE CAREERS • 211

    Motivation   212
    Realities   212
    Research   213
    Resources and Services   214
    Consulting   215
    Temping   218
    Buying a Business   219
    Starting a Business   224
    Making a Transfer to Another Function in Your Company   225
    Working for a Nonprofit or Trade Association   226

17. MAKING THE NEW JOB AND YOUR FUTURE A SUCCESS • 229

    Transition   229
    Getting Started   234
    Plan for the Future   238
    Conclusion   240

Send in for Additional Tips • 241

Index • 243

PREFACE

Most job hunters are carrying out the right activities, but those who aren't making reasonable progress are not doing these activities effectively. In doing this they're underselling themselves. Someone who shoots 100 in golf is trying to hit the same types of shots as someone who shoots par; he or she just isn't hitting them as well. This book shows you how to improve your job hunting score from, say, 100 to about 80.

This improvement occurs in two steps. In the first step, you will become better prepared for your job search by becoming more effective in determining your goals, writing a top-flight resume, gaining access to key people, succeeding in interviews, and dealing with frequent rejections. In the second step, you will apply the newly learned techniques in every step of your job search, while learning from rejections and mistakes.

This book explains in depth many of the techniques top-flight outplacement firms use with their clients. The best firms have developed the most practical and successful techniques for their job hunters to follow. Many of the techniques explained in this book aren't included in other books, or they are not described in enough detail to be really useful. This book describes each step clearly and provides good examples so that you can apply them as you need to.

Among the things you'll learn are how to improve your networking, blind prospecting, approaching recruiters, using the Internet, and answering ads. You'll learn how to be a better salesman of yourself and how to be a better negotiator. You'll also be shown techniques to use your time better, improve your decisions, and become a better self-critic. You'll learn how to gain the most from using the many resources available to job hunters such as job-help workshops, former and current job hunters, executive recruiters, the Internet, key executives, and other sources for their knowledge, moral support, and advice. In Chapter 13, "Conducting an Effective Search," you'll find a checklist to help you evaluate the status of your job search and identify the source of any problems you may be having and some ways to correct these problems.

This book places particular emphasis on networking, and it provides a 12-step program for networking productivity. In DBM's recent survey of over 28,000 job hunters who secured jobs in 2001, 60 percent of the respondents said that networking was the source of their new job. This figure is 74 percent of those whose new job source is identified. Yet most job hunting books don't give instructions on how to improve networking.

HOW TO FIND WHAT YOU'RE LOOKING FOR

There are two ways to use this book. One way is to look over the contents and focus on your specific current interests. Skimming the surface this way may work out. If that's your choice, I hope it does. However, a cursory reading may not help you avoid taking a job that is really not right for you for one reason or another. In my experience, one quarter of the new jobs people take don't work out—in fact, many don't last a year. Are you willing to run this high a risk?

The second approach—the one I highly recommend—is to start by carefully reading the contents, then skimming the whole book to get an understanding of its complete program. Then you should carry out the book's exercises and instructions to prepare a well-organized search, sticking with it until you get an offer that's in line with your job interests and needs at this stage of your career. In time you'll find which of the techniques are most useful for you. The prospect may appear to be a longer search—and it could be, but not necessarily. It does, however, increase the chances considerably of your getting a better fit—and it could even take less time.

ACKNOWLEDGMENTS

I'm grateful to these Outplacement and Human Resources professionals for their wise counsel on the book:

- Robert H. Ellis, Ph.D., Principal, Ellis Management
- James R. Jandl, Vice President Human Resources, Oxford Global Resources, Inc.
- Cynthia A. Sullivan, Principal, Career Strategies, Inc.
- E. Brian Veasy, Senior Marketing Consultant, R. L. Stevens & Associates, Inc.

Others over many years have been a great source of advice and support: Dr. Lee Wotherspoon, Robert M. Armstrong, F. Gordon Brigham, Jr., Neil S. MacKenna, Gail Morrissey, and Ephriam Radner.

I'm grateful to Grace Freedson, who as my agent has been a frequent source of wise advice and strong encouragement. I also appreciate the efforts that Barry Neville, my editor, has made on my behalf. Elizabeth Case, my assistant, has provided help over and above the call of duty.

THE
EXECUTIVE
JOB SEARCH

CHAPTER 1

GETTING PERSPECTIVE

YOU'VE GOT A WONDERFUL OPPORTUNITY

Perhaps you're out of work. Perhaps you're still on a job but you're not happy and about to quit. Perhaps you were in the wrong place at the wrong time, or you missed some of the warning lights on your last job choice.

Whatever. Now you have a crucial choice: Are you looking for just another job, which, if you're lucky, will turn out to be what you really want for the long run, or are you determined to get the job you've dreamed about for a long time, a job that you really like to do, that emphasizes your strengths, that connects you with stimulating people, and that has strong, long-term prospects?

The choice is yours. You can do anything you want.

Does this kind of dream job sound too good to be true? It can be a reality, but you have to work smartly to get this dream job. It may take more work to get a dream job than an ordinary job, and the process may be riskier. But the rewards are far greater.

There are five essentials for success:

- *Have a positive attitude.* People respond more positively to winners than they do to losers.

- *Don't reinvent the wheel.* Millions have carried out job searches before you have, and virtually all have done so successfully. You

1

know quite a few of them. Many can give you good advice and useful resources and techniques. They can also put you in touch with other helpful and supportive people.

• *Be thorough in preparing for your job search.* The preparations described for your search are more comprehensive than in most books. Too many job hunters shortchange themselves on these steps, only to regret it later. Overlap steps to speed things up. For example, while waiting for resume critique feedback, prepare your contact list with addresses and phone numbers.

• *Keep working on improving your job hunting skills in every aspect of your search.*

• *Conduct an active search once you've completed your preparation.* Set a goal of 7 to 10 networking or job interviews a week.

If you haven't read the preface, you'll find that reading it is helpful by describing what the book covers and how to use it most effectively.

COPING WITH LOSING YOUR JOB

The Career Initiatives Center (CIC) is a "career transition services" organization for displaced midcareer job hunters in Cleveland. The first thing they give new candidates is the pamphlet *Coping with Loss* by Robert B. Garber. The pamphlet enumerates the "stages of job-loss crisis" most job hunters go through to varying degrees:

• Shock
• Denial and/or disbelief
• Self-isolation
• Anger
• Bargaining
• Guilt and remorse
• Panic

+ Depression
+ Understanding of and resignation to the situation
+ Acceptance of reality
+ Building a positive outlook
+ Opportunity, growth, and new direction

While the list looks formidable, remember that these feelings are normal and millions have gone through them before you and have survived. You'll find you'll go through most of these stages, a few not even recognizing it, and not always in this exact order. This book will show you how to deal with them by focusing on your future and conducting a very active job search. If you do these two things well, then the stages become manageable.

Whether you were laid off or fired, having negative feelings is normal, but be sure to control them. Work on developing a positive attitude. Don't criticize your ex-employer to others because people who might help will fear your criticism as well.

Develop a positive explanation of why you are "looking." It may be something like "Things were OK, then there were changes [a new boss, your project was a disappointment, or the company slipped overall]. I was just one of the people laid off. Several senior people at XYZ know my work and will give me strong recommendations. With my experience and my capabilities, in time I'm sure I'll find another good job."

There's still some stigma to being out of work, but not as much as there was 20 or 25 years ago. It happens too frequently now and to too many competent and hard-working people. In the old days executive recruiters rarely risked recommending people who had lost their jobs. Today they're considerably more likely to recommend them.

Wanting to vent your anger, fear, and frustration is quite normal. If you have to let it all out, be careful whom you do it with. Approach at most one or two people you trust, people who'll give you permission to do it. Often the best people are those who have been through a difficult midcareer job search themselves.

Feeling uncomfortable in revealing your salary (which you've always kept private) or having to describe some distasteful aspects of your prior jobs is common. Unfortunately providing such personal information is part of the process, but you'll soon get used to doing so.

You'll probably feel awkward socializing at parties, community meetings, or church. You can manage such circumstances by identifying people that you feel comfortable with and socializing with them. Such casual acquaintances can often provide networking interviews. Inevitably you'll run into a few people who want to pry. Decline to answer their questions. Change the subject or walk away. Their prying tells more about them than it does about you.

YOU'VE GOT A LOT GOING FOR YOU

You took certain things for granted when you were employed. Now that you're "in between," those things may not seem so positive. The things themselves haven't changed; recognize that it's your perspective that has. Let's look at a few of these things and think about how important they are in your whole scheme of things:

- Your family or partner strengthens the central core of your being and is greatly satisfying.
- You have had many years of experience in various roles and have produced a credible record, which, if properly marketed, will be attractive to several good employers.
- You've developed many skills that earned you your recent, important position. These skills will be useful in your job search and in your future.
- You have a circle of friends who are important to you. Some of them will help you at this time.

- The organizations that you belong to, such as church and community groups, have satisfied you and have broadened your horizons, and they may also help you during this search.
- Your hobbies and outside interests have always given you pleasure and have broadened your experiences.
- Your material possessions fulfill you.

Even though you're uncertain at this time, look around you and remember all the people you've seen leave one job and find a new job similar to or better than the old one. You'll get a good job too, although it will take some hard work and will undoubtedly cause much frustration.

Losing a job is a major loss—of income, of opportunity to get experience, and of time. On the other hand, it isn't a complete loss. Rather, it's an opportunity to assess your values and goals and to become more realistic about them. It's an opportunity to get your life back on track, to make conscious choices that will move you closer to your goals. It's an opportunity to improve your skills of selling yourself, of making decisions, and of managing your job search —all of which will be useful in your new job and in your personal life in the future. You have a chance to be more creative and more assertive, to ask for support, to expand your horizons, and finally, when it's all over, to have made new friends and broadened your network.

GETTING THINGS IN FOCUS

Some people describe job hunting as "selling yourself." There's no question this is a key aspect of the process. In selling yourself, you inevitably get rejected a lot. Even those who are highly sought after get rejected. Adding this rejection to your negative feelings about leaving your last job can discourage you. Think of rejection as a bump in the road, and remember that you're moving in the right direction.

When facing a job search, which is difficult under the best of circumstances, many job hunters undersell themselves. A key feature of

5

this book is that it can help you develop skills to overcome this tendency and help you become a more effective job hunter.

When you first tried to ride a bike, you probably fell off many times. Through trial and error, eventually you learned how to stay on it. A month or two later you were probably racing your buddies. Similarly, when you made your first presentation to a boss, you probably made mistakes, but, over time, as you made more presentations, you got more convincing. Now you're job hunting—which is something you've probably done several times before. But this time, because you're now midcareer, it's tougher. Many of the jobs you seek have been eliminated, so there's more competition for the few remaining jobs. The following strategies can help you:

+ Are you willing to settle for "just another job," or are you determined to find the job you deserve, one that really turns you on? In commenting about Americans, Winston Churchill once said, "You can always get them [Americans] to do the right thing after they have exhausted all the other possibilities," (*Finding Work Without Losing Heart—Bouncing Back from Mid-career Job Loss*, William J. Bryan, SJ, Adams Publishing, 1995). Make it easy on yourself. Do the right thing the first time around. Start your search with a careful self-assessment, as described in Chapter 3, "Determining Your Job Goals."

+ Select two or three trusted friends to act as advisors on your job search. Find people you're confident in, and you can talk to every few weeks about your progress, and who will be accessible on short notice for advice on major decisions.

+ Join a job search workshop. You can learn a lot participating in a good one. It's a comfort seeing other capable people "in the same boat" with whom you can develop mutual support. Just disregard the naysayers.

- Seek out successful job hunters who may have useful ideas from their own experience and know of good resources and helpful people. Ask them what they have found most helpful in staying upbeat during this unsettling period.

- Talk with friends who are successful salespeople, because they're experts in many of the techniques you need to conduct a successful search, such as getting appointments, presenting yourself, and dealing with roadblocks.

- Practice on some mediocre contacts before you see the key contacts so that you don't blow your best opportunities. The best outplacement firms don't let their candidates see anyone until they have completed two to three weeks of intensive preparation.

- You may be rejected because of who you are, your background, or how you present yourself. Analyze each rejection, and learn what you can do better in your next job interview or networking meeting.

- Avoid job hunters with a negative attitude, because they might drag you down.

- Don't set unrealistic goals. For example, in phoning for appointments, don't expect the same success you had on your last job, in which you dealt with many of the same people regularly. It's more realistic to compare this week's success rate with last week's. This same advice applies to other job search activities.

- Reward yourself for a good effort, even though the results may be disappointing. You're entitled to a reward such as watching one of your children's games (where you might be able to network), playing golf or tennis, having a social lunch or coffee with a friend, or spending time on a favorite project.

- Get exercise. Take a long walk or play tennis or swim. Exercise reduces stress and provides diversion.

- Lead as normal a life as you can. Continue with your pleasurable activities, but cut back on the frills. (Go to a less fancy restaurant and less often.)
- Make sure you dress appropriately for all networking and job interviews.
- Make sure your hair styling is reasonable—even if it takes color touch.
- Project a high energy level, appearing as fit as possible and getting enough sleep.
- Don't overindulge. Limit your drinking and eating.
- Ask for help, even though it's uncomfortable to do sometimes.
- Accept negative results as inevitable, and learn from them.
- Take every opportunity to meet people. One job hunter went reluctantly to his wife's 25th high school reunion, and while he was there, he met someone who became a close associate for the rest of his career. If you encounter people who have a "holier-than-thou" attitude, remember that they may be knocking on your door in a year or two asking for your help.

HOW MUCH OF A FACTOR IS YOUR AGE?

Most job hunters in their midforties and older have more difficulty in their job search than they did earlier in their careers. It's easy to blame this difficulty on age because of our culture's negative perceptions about age in the workplace. Although age may add some difficulty, job hunters often overestimate its effect. You can reduce the effect of your age on your job search by dealing with it specifically.

How much age affects your job search depends on whether you seek a traditional position with a company or an alternative career. In a traditional position, age may exert a major or minor effect, depending on the company's needs, its culture, and your experience.

In an alternative career, age may be less of a factor, and in fact, being older can be an asset.

Unless you're sure which choice you want, the traditional position or an alternative career, take advantage of your wonderful opportunity by exploring both options. You may see this exploration as only prolonging your job search, but it may, in fact, speed things up—and it may reach a more satisfactory long-term solution. This job search may enable you to "reframe yourself" into a role much more to your liking at this stage of your life.

If your choice is to seek a traditional position with a company, do you want a large and conservative company or a small and free-wheeling one? How age affects this decision depends on the company's culture, its needs, your experience, and your behavior. Age won't be a major deterrent if you convince management, particularly your prospective boss, that you're the best and the safest candidate for the job. Some companies particularly like midcareer workers because they've "been there" in many situations and know things younger workers just don't know yet.

Many companies, particularly in the technology fields are dominated, however, by a youth culture. Older job hunters must convince the key people in these companies not only that their skills are state of the art but also that their outlook and behavior will be accepted by other, particularly younger, employees.

If you are considering an alternative career, it may be one of the following options:

- Consulting
- Working for a nonprofit organization, such as a trade association
- A traditional job but in a different functional area (e.g., operations instead of finance)
- Several part-time jobs
- Temping

- Starting a business
- Buying an existing business

Each of these options has pros and cons that you need to evaluate based on your experience, your financial needs, and the risks you're willing to take. (See Chapter 16, "Alternative Careers.")

DEALING WITH A RAPIDLY CHANGING WORLD

High technology in the world of work has changed the workplace dramatically in recent years. This trend will undoubtedly accelerate and spread. In the 1990s dot.coms and related small high-technology companies were emerging and evolving so rapidly that the greatest growth in jobs was in this economic sector. A lot of those companies have since fallen by the wayside, but their influence has persisted and has changed how most businesses are run. More and more, larger companies are under pressure to show ever-improving quarterly earnings. To meet that demand for continuous growth, larger companies have been forced to adopt new technology just to survive.

Along with the high-technology innovations have come other significant changes in the work world, changes that have been economically or politically motivated such as the increasing government regulation of some industries and the deregulation of others. Technology changes have yielded many new products and services, such as the Internet and the Wal-Mart type of product distribution. In addition, globalization has dramatically increased the type and extent of business dealings in foreign markets.

These changes have made companies reorganize. Many companies have revised their key missions, have adopted techniques such as streamlining through total quality management (TQM), reengineering, have hired both basic and contingent work forces, and have learned to treat internal constituencies as customers. Emphasis has shifted from process to productivity. And a new breed of managers has evolved who can operate across functions in a loosely structured organization set up in project teams.

You've probably already been affected by this new environment: You're expected to get more done with less, to operate efficiently despite constant change and loose functional lines, to be a team player, to make decisions in a group context, to use diverse team members, to think in terms of overall systems, to foresee how your goals are affected by these changes, and finally to get others to adapt to these changes.

What has this new environment meant for you? You've learned to be sharper and more flexible, and able to work effectively with all kinds of coworkers. You've refined your values, skills, and interests. You've focused on your next step and prepared yourself for it. You've used your unique skills to contribute to the company's goals. You've kept current on the new technology by developing a diverse network with a wide knowledge base. If you're older than most of your associates, keeping your knowledge at a state-of-the-art level is essential, as is working smoothly with various types of people, particularly younger people, and developing a good rapport with them. What you've experienced so far is bound to continue.

GETTING WHAT'S YOURS

When you leave a company, one of the first things you must deal with is getting all you're entitled to. Until a decade or so ago, there was considerable room for negotiation with the company over severance benefits. Recently, however, most companies have shifted to offering fixed severance packages. Don't accept this, however, as a fact without testing it. Make an effort to understand your benefits and all your options.

The largest dollar item in the package is usually severance pay. It's most often set by a formula based on your length of service and the level of your position. Your best chance to increase severance pay may be asking for an extension if you're still job searching when the benefits run out, particularly if you can demonstrate you've been conducting an aggressive job search.

Getting outplacement services used to be somewhat negotiable, but rarely is it anymore. Many companies provide only token outplacement services, if any, except for the most senior executives. *Good* counseling can be extremely useful (see Chapter 2, "Getting Off to a Good Start"), so be sure to ask about this option, including your right to select the firm.

Obtain a clear statement of what kind of reference the company is willing to give you. Many companies officially give only a minimal statement that you worked for the company for a certain period at a certain salary. Therefore, try to get one or two senior associates in the company to act as references, hopefully to explain that you were laid off because of a difficult situation basically beyond your control.

Other severance benefits can involve complicated options. You may be entitled to medical insurance, unemployment insurance, retirement benefits, vacation pay, profit sharing and bonuses, 401(k)s, and disability and life insurance. Make sure you understand the options, and get advice from someone experienced with these benefits or, as a last resort, from a lawyer who specializes in such matters.

Even if you have been mistreated by the company, do not bring legal action against it. You'll probably lose. The action can use up valuable money, time, and energy that you would better spend on getting another job. Plus, taking legal action could result in a blot on your employability.

The free pamphlet *The Benefits of Being Laid Off,* by Priscilla H. Claman and published by Career Strategies and most recently updated in 2001, explains these benefits and is worth getting. It can be obtained from Career Strategies, Inc., by calling (617) 227-5517 or by e-mailing info@career-strategies.com or visiting their Web site at career-strategies.com.

CHAPTER 2

GETTING OFF TO A GOOD START

WHY A GOOD START IS IMPORTANT

You may have lost your job recently. When you woke up the next morning, you realized that for the first time perhaps in years you have a completely open schedule. You had been working under a lot of pressure, but now you have received this setback to your career and to your ego. Isn't this time for a vacation?

No. Take a week to relax and get organized, but don't postpone the job search. You've got a major task ahead of you, and the sooner you get on with it, the sharper you'll be. If you fall off a horse, you're told to get back on the horse right away, to put the fall behind you. Follow that advice. You can take a vacation before you start your next job, but your top priority right now is to find that next one. Furthermore, being busy at your job search will get you over the shock of being laid off and help get you back on a payroll sooner.

If you're still working and haven't decided to leave, read Chapter 15, "Should You Make a Job Change?"

Bill Martin was just about to leave his company forever when he got a call from Sam Fulton, a good friend who had an excellent reputation for helping executives get new jobs. Sam had lined up an interview for him for a very good position for two days from then. Sam signed off by saying that Bill had to bring an up-to-date resume to the interview. The interview didn't go well. Several months later, Bill was still using the same resume, which, he finally realized, wasn't working. Bill then revised his resume with the help of a successful job hunter. Within a month he had appointments for nine interviews, resulting in five offers. In retrospect, Bill realized he'd had lost a lot of time and probably the best help from his most influential contacts by not being well prepared at the beginning of his campaign. Bill would have been better off if he had used his first resume as a temporary one until he had done the careful preparation work, including getting his resume properly critiqued, as described in Chapter 6, "Making Your Resume an Effective Tool."

IMPROVING YOUR MENTAL OUTLOOK

Whether you have been fired or laid off or you left by your own choice, you're now in an uncertain position. At this stage, some people need to justify themselves, and they do so by bad-mouthing their former employer. This is a great mistake. People don't want to hear such complaints. They may think less of you for it, wondering whether you will also criticize your next employer (or even themselves). This advice applies to conversations you have with family and friends as well, because they may have good job leads for you but even they might hesitate to give them to you if they think you will be critical of your next employer too. A key to a successful job search is having a positive attitude. Put all your negative thoughts behind you; if you can't manage that, at least don't give voice to them publicly.

AVOIDING PITFALLS

There are many ways to make mistakes in a job search. Let's look at some and learn how to avoid them.

- Many job hunters hurt their chances by not planning carefully and not working vigorously. You can bypass that trap by using this book as a good outplacement counselor who is continuously at your elbow. Follow its instructions carefully. It will help you speed up the process and develop better options. *Start your planning now.*

- A job search is strictly self-initiated. Many people will help when you approach them, but rarely will anyone volunteer. *Your progress depends on your efforts.* The sooner you move ahead aggressively on your preparation, the better off you'll be.

- *Don't count on promises.* In the first week of his job search Fred got an interview with a well-established company in his industry. At the end of the interview, the interviewer said, "We're extremely interested in you, Fred. I'm going to arrange for a second interview." At the second interview, the interviewer said, "We want to hire you for this particular position. I just have to clear this with my boss, and I'll get back to you in a few days." Fred was very pleased, but never heard from this company again, and he got a cool reception each time he followed up. This happens frequently. So don't count on anything until you have a firm offer, preferably in writing. Act as though the possibility doesn't exist, and continue prospecting actively.

- *Don't waste your best contacts.* Sam and Bill had been members of a weekly golf foursome for years, and they had become good friends. When Sam lost his job, he immediately called Bill, a much more senior executive at another company. Bill was cordial and happy to help. Sam made the mistake of thinking his social relationship with Bill would open several doors. He was unprepared for the meeting and made a poor impression. Frankly, Bill feared that Sam would make a similarly poor impression on his best contacts, whom he cherished and protected. Bill did refer Sam to a couple of medium-level people, but Sam was disappointed. When Sam contacted Bill for further help, Bill scarcely returned his calls. This mistake of spoiling good contacts happens frequently when job hunters don't conduct themselves professionally.

- *Don't blindly accept advice.* In making the rounds of people you know and those they refer you to, you'll get lots of advice. Some of it will be good, and some of it won't be. Through a referral, Frank was granted an interview with Mary, the Vice President of Human Resources of XYZ. Mary strongly recommended that Frank not undertake the intensive target mailing he had planned. Frank did the mailing anyway, and the letter to the CFO of XYZ within a month got him a very good offer. Carefully evaluate the advice that you get. Some of it may be unintentionally biased, misleading, or downright wrong. If you're in doubt about a piece of advice, test it with a couple of other people you see.

- *Be careful about repeating the same mistakes.* A job search is repetitive. Much of your activity is geared to gaining access to key people and to making as favorable an impression as possible. It's easy to "get in a groove" and present yourself the same way over and over again, whether your presentation is effective or not. Evaluate responses to your presentation, and change it accordingly. Respond to your "gut" feeling. Experiment when the risk is low, such as in an occasional networking interview. You may find a revised presentation considerably more effective.

- *Don't ignore your financial situation.* If your job search goes on a long time, finances can become a major problem. Many job hunters think they'll get a new job faster than they actually do. So early on, examine your finances carefully and develop a contingency plan in case of a long search. Decide what personal expenses you can reduce or postpone. You may be able to defer some major bills, such as mortgages, insurance bills, and college tuition. Approach the companies well in advance and explain your circumstances. Don't be too proud to accept unemployment compensation. Record your expenses in the job search carefully because many of them are tax deductible.

♦ *Don't give up developing new prospects until you accept your new job.* It's easy to get trapped into letting up on your efforts when you're waiting for a decision from one or more good prospects. Psychologically you're better off to keep the pressure on to maintain your momentum because first, it keeps you busy and mentally sharp, and second, prospects can cool off quickly and leave you facing the difficult task of having to restart your prospecting.

DEALING WITH YOUR FAMILY

Job hunting by the major breadwinner in the family affects each member, but differently. A nonworking spouse or partner is particularly vulnerable. An understanding spouse or partner can be a great asset in a job search. Discuss the job search frequently and be candid. Develop a good give-and-take about the future, about your and your partner's feelings, your finances, your progress in the search, the possibility of moving to another location, and the interests of any children. Have this kind of chat at least every couple of weeks.

The spouse has little control over the job search but is very much affected by it. The spouse may find a confidant helpful, especially one who is the spouse of a former job hunter.

It's important for the job hunter and partner to express their love for each other frequently during this stressful time. Spend time together. Have fun together. Socialize, exercise, or just hang out.

Don't overlook the effect of this period on the children, including the younger ones. They may be more affected than you think. A former CEO was offered a dollar by his six-year-old (proceeds from his lemonade stand) because, "he might need it at this time." Teenagers often feel their way of life threatened, particularly if there is a chance of relocation. Discuss with the children in an appropriate way what's going on, and listen to their concerns. Explain that the breadwinner is under strain and is working hard to get another job.

Point out that people lose their jobs frequently today, through no fault of their own. Explain that you did a good job, but you got laid off anyway. Furthermore, explain that it's your goal to minimize the upset of the job change and that you're trying to find a job locally. Also tell them it often takes a long time to get the "right" job, and accepting something less might possibly make all the family losers.

GOOD COUNSELING CAN BE A GREAT HELP

In the last two decades, the amount of job and outplacement counseling has increased greatly. Most people find job counseling helpful, although some individuals have had bad experiences. Sometimes the failures are because the job hunter doesn't work hard or resourcefully enough at using what the counseling could provide. Fortunately, poor experiences are far outnumbered by those who have found their counseling to be valuable, often extremely so. Given the financial risks of a job search in midcareer, counseling may be a wise investment. A good counselor can speed up the process of getting a new job, of evaluating job options, and finally of making a sensible choice.

The best outplacement services guide you in several activities:

- Reviewing your experience, job objective, and priorities to help you identify your best options
- Presenting your accomplishments in the best way in a resume, in a cover letter, on the phone, and in interviews
- Developing strategies and techniques for finding job leads by approaching recruiters, the Internet, network contacts, and companies directly

- Improving skills in dealing with problems and tough questions
- Demonstating how to use the Internet and other sources to find job openings, help, and information on companies
- Improving techniques of telephoning, interviewing, networking, and blind prospecting
- Providing a sense of belonging with others in similar circumstances, which can often can be mutually beneficial as people exchange leads, ideas, and resources
- Providing access to their successful client alumni and alumnae
- Evaluating and negotiating offers and making the final decision

Finding a good counselor for a reasonable fee may not be easy. Most counselors charge a flat fee covering all services until you get a new job, although some offer a reduced fee for limited help. Because of the increase in the number of counselors, many of them negotiate fees. A few charge by the hour, which can benefit you. Research counselors carefully through your network.

Learn the value of counseling and the identity of the best counselors. Meet with a counselor to decide whether you'll be comfortable working together. Ask candid questions, such as his or her rate of failures and the reasons for some of them. Ask for references from former clients (unsuccessful ones as well as successful ones). Follow up and question each of these referrals critically. If you decide to use a counselor, choose someone based on the personal chemistry between you, information provided by referrals, and the fee.

Don't be put off by time spent in searching for a good counselor. Having a good counselor should reduce the actual job search time while increasing the number of your choices.

ORGANIZE TO WORK EFFICIENTLY

Set up your office so that it's efficient and free from interference. A busy spouse may load you up with household chores because you're

19

not working. This work is piled on top of your full-time job—getting another one. Demonstrate that you're working at your search full time by actually doing so. If you have a laptop and a cell phone, there's little need to spend much search time at home. If you have a desktop computer, you may have to work from your home, unless a friend will lend you a desk and phone in his office, in which case, you can set up your office including your computer, in his.

RECORD KEEPING

An important activity is to maintain control over the "paperwork" an aggressive campaign requires. The preparation phase of your search can easily be done by setting up manual files. However, if you conduct an active networking and blind prospecting campaign, keeping your records manually becomes cumbersome. So you're better off from the start doing your record keeping on your computer. Get the advice of several recent or current job hunters or a good workshop on how to set it up best.

CHAPTER 3

DETERMINING YOUR JOB GOALS

This chapter will help you choose your job goals logically. It does this by showing you how to consider the following factors:

* The phases of a typical career
* Who you are
* Your likes and dislikes
* Your five to seven top job priorities
* Your alternative career possibilities
* Your actual job choice

CAREER PHASES

Most careers go through the stages shown in Exhibit 3-1. Keep the stages in mind. Don't be misled by the publicity that has been given to a few extremely successful executives and entrepreneurs.

When you graduated and started working, your goal may have been to "make it to the top" however you visualized your dream objective. That is a common goal at this stage of life. Now that you are well established in your career, you have recognized that "making to the top" is no longer likely. Nevertheless, you've had a successful

EXHIBIT 3-1 • Phases of a Typical Career

	General Age Range			
	Early 20s–Late 20s	Late 20s–Early 40s	Early 40s–Retirement	Late 40s and throughout 50s –Retirement
Career stage	Early development	Advanced development	Top responsibility	Possible final promotion or second career to pursue other interests
Objective	To identify your career choice and to develop basic skills	To develop in-depth expertise in your field	To utilize your expertise in your major job	To select your role for your final career phase
Typical characteristics	• Indoctrination into the world of full-time work • Development of basic job skills • Broadening of your horizons to learn a variety of options for accomplishing your career goals and general requirements for them • Several promotions • Several job changes	• Deciding finally on your chosen career (early in this phase) • Increasing exposure to other company functions through interrelated problems • Intense pressure to produce and to grow professionally • A couple of less frequent but very important promotions	• Your maximum responsibility (perhaps one promotion in the future) • Often general or administrative management rather than functional management • Broadening of your field of interests by community committees	A new career could: • Take a variety of forms, which are a major change from the prior career • Fulfill a desire to do something you want to do while you can • Occur in a much less structured environment so you can pursue other interests (community activities, travel, etc. • Be at lower compensation (most of the cost of raising family over) • Enable you to pursue a second career indefinitely (overcoming fixed retirement age of most companies)

career and, most recently, a good job. At midcareer, your goals for the rest of your work life can take several directions, for example:

♦ To find another job like your last one but with better prospects

♦ To do something very different via an alternative career

By the early forties, most people's careers approach a plateau. You may still advance, but your advancement will be slower than it was earlier in your career. Instead of moving up the corporate pyramid, you may advance by broadening your responsibilities in your current role. Your best chance for immediate advancement is with another company at a riskier job, a job you may be leery of. At this stage, without the promise of rapid advancement, you may have thought about doing something quite different but not considered it seriously because giving up your existing job seemed too drastic. In your midforties and beyond, your financial demands probably seem more achievable: assuming you have your children's educational expenses and your mortgage on a manageable plan. Your spouse or partner may be paying a major share of the household expenses. Your main concern now is providing for a comfortable retirement. At this stage, if you've been considering a career change, don't rule it out.

THE SEARCH PROCESS

Now let's look at the decision process you'll be going through that will lead to your next job. Exhibit 3-2, "Job Choice Steps for Tom Franks," shows the normal job search process. For most people in their midcareer, particularly those who find themselves in a job search through no fault of their own, choosing a career takes little thought. They know they want the same career and a position similar to their last one but with a few improvements, such as a job one step up the ladder with better prospects at a better company. For those who want to do something quite different, the step of choosing a career is important. Once having made your choice of career, the next

EXHIBIT 3-2 • Job Choice Steps for Tom Franks, Age 45, Marketing Director, 400 Employees, McNeil Networks

	Career Choice		Job Choice	
	Research	Decision	Job Search	Decision
Stage	Evaluation of career alternatives	Decision on most desirable career	Search for job alternatives	Decision on most desirable job offer
Procedure	Research on each career (personal interviews and reading)	Evaluation of career alternatives	Job search resulting in offers for specific jobs	Evaluation of specific offers

Options	Management consulting
	
	Buying a small business
	
	Marketing executive
	
	Sales executive
		Marketing Executive	Reliance Networks:
			  Marketing Director
			ANV:
			  Technical Sales &
			  Marketing Specialist
			Monarch Communications:
			  Marketing Planning
			  Specialist
				ANV:
				Technical Sales and Marketing Specialist

step for *all* job hunters is to choose the job itself. During this step, ideally you should develop several job offers from which to choose. You'll make a better choice this way usually.

JOB GOALS

Now let's determine your job goals, which consist of two items:

• *Your job objective.* The term *your objective* is conventionally used to mean your answer to questions like "What do you want to do?" or "What are you looking for?"

• *Your priorities.* These are the five to seven criteria you use in making career decisions. Examples of these criteria follow:

  • Stability of the company and the job

  • Compatible work environment

  • Compatible philosophy and values

- Avoiding relocation
- Fair compensation with reasonable future prospects
- Your liking of the actual tasks and responsibilities of the job

In determining your job goals, asking the opinion of one or two carefully chosen friends and your spouse or partner of what they think would be most suitable may be extremely helpful. This is especially true at the three decision points in this process, so try to review your thinking with a trusted friend at each of them: self-assessment and determining your priorities, alternative career analysis, and alternative job analysis.

This book treats the situation of changing functional areas, for example, from a career in finance to a career in operations in your company. If you are considering a functional change elsewhere, consider using a career counselor. This book also treats starting an alternative career, such as consulting, temping, or starting or buying a business. These options are discussed in Chapter 16, "Alternative Careers."

JOB PRIORITIES

Determining five to seven priorities can be complicated.

Gus Rivers was a successful executive who found himself out of a job at the age of 43. In contemplating his priorities, he said, "My wife wants me to be the company president." This statement tells a lot. It doesn't say, "I want to be president," nor does it say, "My wife wants me to be successful" or "happy" or "challenged"—or even "to earn big bucks." Whether he shared his wife's wish for him to be the president or not, he had to contend with it. Some job hunters make key decisions based more on emotions than on logic—sometimes with dire results. This chapter helps you make choices logically.

Many job holders didn't persevere long enough or use good judgment on their last job search. Job counselors work with many individuals in that predicament. Many years ago, I had 11 clients whose degrees were from prestigious graduate schools and who had apparently successful careers. They came to me for help because each of them had taken a job in the last year that had not worked out. All of them felt they had done a careful job search and had made a good choice at the time. Two of them had moved their families to distant locations. All the jobs failed within a year. Three of these job hunters realized on the first day of their new job that they never should have accepted it. How can a successful and intelligent person make such an error? It happens more often than you might think.

In my experience, I have found that at least a quarter of new jobs end in less than a year. Sometimes the break is the company's choice, sometimes it is the employee's, and often it is by mutual consent. The frequent failure of new jobs is confirmed by William J. Morin, founder and former chief executive officer of Drake, Beam, Morin, one of the largest outplacement firms in the country. Morin noted the risks involved in changing jobs in *The Directory of Executive Recruiters* (Kennedy Information, Inc., Peterborough, NH, 1991).

Many individuals who are terminated after 5, 10, or 15 years with a company have a tendency to go out, find a job, and get themselves in trouble quickly in their new position. They bounce from that job on to the next job, and they experience this bouncing for a number of years, because they didn't take the time to ascertain what they did wrong in the position from which they were first fired and to honestly determine the proper work environment in which they would be successful.

Most job hunters try to "ascertain what they did wrong" and "determine the proper work environment," and they genuinely believe they have done so. They have trouble, however, because being realistic in self-appraisal is difficult. This chapter shows you how to conduct an orderly self-appraisal, thus improving your chances of doing it successfully.

Who Are You?

To determine your objectives in your job search and in your life, you must first analyze who you are. Start by summarizing the facts of your current situation. Include your current or former job status, your age, your education, your experience, your last salary, your financial needs, your financial resources, your skills, your interests, your deficiencies, your preferred work environment, your family's desired lifestyle, and other personal facts. Establish your primary requirements for a job. Don't undervalue your preferred work environment and your desired lifestyle because they can be critical to your satisfaction and long-term success. It is human nature to look for a new job that corrects the deficiencies of the old one and to play down the attractive features of your last job, important things that were right in the old job. Don't overcompensate for deficiencies. Consider all these issues, and weigh them appropriately. See Tom Franks's answer to "Who are you?" shown in Exhibit 3-3.

Knowing what you can and cannot do is important in planning your career. A good example is Paul, who is a successful entrepreneur. Over 15 or 20 years he took four small, struggling companies and straightened them out. After he switched to a new company several years ago, I asked him, "Why didn't you stay with Company A? It seemed to be going very well." He answered clearly, "Well, I learned something about myself a long time ago. I have a particular type of expertise, and I recognize my own limitations. I do best getting a company up to about $15 million or so in sales. After that the company needs a different kind of management. I'm much more effective—and more excited—building up small companies than managing larger ones." Paul has been successful, and he has had a satisfying career, largely because of his realistic attitude. Not only does he recognize exactly what his expertise is but also what his limitations are. Furthermore, he has accepted them.

EXHIBIT 3-3 • Self-Assessment for Tom Franks

73 Bellevue Drive, Glendale, Il.

Age 45

Married, 3 children ages 17, 16, 14

Georgia Tech, AB, 1978, Mechanical Engineering Honors

Two years as Sergeant in the Infantry in Vietnam

Twenty-one years' marketing and sales; most recently marketing director of a 200-employee telecommunications company.

Salary $95,000; bonus 5%

No outside income now or in prospect

Pension accumulation; has IRA with value of $137,000

Investments $150,000 (one-half earmarked for children's college expenses)

Receiving 3 months' severance

Wife earns $42,000 per year running clothes shop

House valued at $300,000; 60% paid for

Strengths	Excellent knowledge of product; handles most customers well. Prefers planning to line supervision. Excellent problem solver. Supervisor of technical specialists.
Weaknesses	Weak at company politics. Doesn't like confrontation (i.e., dealing with unhappy customers). Detail minded. Likes a controlled environment.
Personal	Has lost job twice (both times company got in trouble). Wife has spent whole life in area and would be very upset by move, as would children. Is a homebody. Principal interests are family, home, and community (has been active in community). Active gardener and golfer.

Finding out what you can do and cannot do is crucial in determining your career requirements.

Job Responsibilities and Environment

You'll do best and be happiest in a job that is consistent with your personal interests and values and that emphasizes your strengths and deemphasizes your weaknesses. In midcareer, you can narrow or broaden your responsibilities in your field. You can seek new challenges. Take this opportunity to question yourself about the options:

* Are you happier in a big company or a small one?
* Are you happier in a stable, conservative company or a riskier small company or startup?
* Are there particular industries that you are well suited for or that you should avoid?
* Do you prefer to be in a staff or a line role?
* Would you rather be a specialist in a particular field or have broader management responsibilities?
* What kind of people (particularly your boss) would you prefer to work with or avoid?
* How important is the company's prestige?
* How important is your title?
* How important are good chances for promotion?
* What kind of management style are you happiest under: loosely or highly structured?
* What sorts of risks are you willing to take?
* Is developing opportunities now for after retirement important to you?

You may be offered a job in a troubled situation, which probably entails considerable risk. Many people get in trouble on their jobs, not because of their own incompetence but because of circumstances beyond their control. When a company is unstable, the performance standards for key people are ordinarily higher than they are in a stable company. For example, the more volatile the situation, the more likely you are to get a new boss with different expectations, jeopardizing your position.

Financial Considerations

The financial aspects of an employment situation can be complex: immediate salary versus long-term earning potential; risk tolerance; realistic potential benefits from incentives and options; medical insurance and retirement benefits. As your future working years are fewer in midcareer and beyond, retirement benefits and the possibility of building a nest egg are more important.

Your Lifestyle

Most people don't decide on a new job just because of the job itself. It's important when choosing a career and a job to focus on your family's needs and your preferred lifestyle and values. Where and how you and your family want to live are extremely important factors. Sometimes no job is worth a move from a place that has been happy for you and your family. Lots of travel, long hours, and undue pressure can affect you and your family, whether or not you still have children at home. You should also consider the opportunity to pursue interests that may become more important to you as retirement approaches.

Look at your work experience and your community involvement to help clarify your priorities. Analyze each position for what you like doing, what environments you've been most happy in, and what kinds of people you've been most comfortable with. As shown in Tom's analysis in Exhibit 3-4, your analysis reveals things you should seek and things you should avoid in a job. The net result isn't always clear, but the analysis will be very helpful.

EXHIBIT 3-4 • Strong Likes and Dislikes for Tom Franks

List each job you've held. What things did you really like and dislike about each job? Your task is to find a job that includes most of your strong likes with the fewest dislikes—both in terms of your activities and the work environment. Including one or two important community activities may also be helpful. Some of the things to consider are the following:

Company's prospects	Your boss
Personal satisfaction	Career development
Work environment	Lifestyle considerations
Compensation and benefits	Coworkers

Rank in priority order which of your likes and dislikes you feel strongest about.

1. McNeil Networks, Marketing Director, 1997–2003

Likes	*Dislikes*
Learned a lot	Company in turmoil
First boss great—left me alone	Second boss was a sneak
Accomplished a lot first 3 years	Lack of cooperation generally
	Lots of politics

2. Fraser Software, VP Marketing, 1993–1997

Likes	*Dislikes*
Being a major player in company	Worked very long hours
Potential of options (never realized)	Company struggling
Lots of autonomy	Marketing role was really selling
	No raises in 3 years; company losing money

3. Commercial Communications, Marketing Manager, 1987–1992

Likes	*Dislikes*
Company stability	Had to move to Texas—didn't want to move
Good support for my ideas	
Annual raises	Company environment deteriorated overnight with new CEO
First boss was great teacher and good guy	1 1/4-hour commute each way
	Second boss was a micromanager

EXHIBIT 3-4 • Strong Likes and Dislikes for Tom Franks *(continued)*

---

4. Franchise TV—then Norton Cable, VP Marketing, 1983–1987

Likes
First 2 years were in forefront
  of technology
Lots of informal perks

Dislikes
Lack of direction from above
Company unable to compete against
  bigger ones
Frustrating atmosphere with lots
  of turnover
Expertise not being developed
Merger led to my being downsized

5. Church Director of Every Member Canvas, 1994

Likes
Had almost complete autonomy
Worked with great group
Exceeded best year to date by 12%

Dislikes
Very demanding on top of heavy
  work schedule

In addition, when analyzing your likes and dislikes, bear in mind that the same factor can be a plus or a minus (e.g. stability and turmoil). Grade factors and tally the results. The following are particularly important for Tom Franks:

Strong company
Good boss
Compatible environment
Fair compensation
Does not want to move
Prefers marketing to selling
Reasonable hours

Make a list of your top priorities for the job you're seeking. Then select the five to seven most important items and put them in order, the most important first. To make his list, Tom compared each priority with each of the other six to determine its relative importance to him. He used the Evaluation of Priorities table, shown in Exhibit 3-5. For example, he decided a "comparatively stable company (1)" was more important than "keeping skills current (2)," so he circled (1). "Fair compensation (6)" was more important than "weaknesses minimized (4)"—so he circled (6). When he completed the comparisons, he counted the number of times each number was circled to determine the importance of each item. He then ranked the results. You can double check the results by putting each of the seven items on an index card and then prioritizing them by gut feel.

Tom took this exercise one step further and put the items in order of importance, and then he analyzed his thinking behind each item, as shown in Exhibit 3-6. When you've completed your job priorities summary, review it carefully with a trusted friend.

During your job search, you will be exposed to various people and job possibilities, and those experiences are apt to change several of your priorities. You may drop some priorities off the list entirely and add others to it. This change is healthy because it represents your becoming more realistic about your true needs. Top compensation is often ranked first on a job hunter's initial priority list, but several months later, it's usually less important and is described as "reasonable compensation with good prospects of future increases." Too many people have been enticed by high compensation into a job that soon fails, leaving the job hunter worse off in the long run.

The two priorities that often top the list well into a job search are a compatible environment and a comparatively stable company. While there are far fewer stable companies today than there were a decade or more ago, it is still possible to find such companies.

EXHIBIT 3-5 • Prioritizing Job Requirements for Tom Franks

	1 Comparatively Stable Company	2 Keep Skills Current	3 Prefers Marketing to Sales	4 Minimizes Weaknesses	5 No Location Move	6 Fair Compensation	7 Compatible Environment
1. Comparatively stable company							
2. Keep skills current	(1) 2						
3. Prefers marketing to sales	(1) 3	2 (3)					
4. Minimizes weaknesses	(1) 4	(2) 4	(3) 4				
5. No location move	(1) 5	2 (5)	3 (5)	4 (5)			
6. Fair compensation	(1) 6	2 (6)	3 (6)	4 (6)	(5) 6		
7. Compatible environment	(1) 7	2 (7)	3 (7)	4 (7)	5 (7)	(6) 7	
Tally score for each winning (circled) factor	6	1	2	0	5	4	3

Tally	Rank	
6	1	Comparative stability
5	2	No location change
4	3	Fair compensation
3	4	Compatible environment
2	5	Prefers marketing to sales
1	6	Keep skills current
0	7	Minimize weaknesses

EXHIBIT 3-6 • Job Priorities Summary for Tom Franks

Priority	Reasoning
Comparatively stable company	Having lost his job twice in the last 6 years, he feels it's critical to be employed for the next 7 years to complete his children's education. Realizes company stability exists much less today than formerly, but it is still available in some companies.
No location change	A move to a different location would be very traumatic now for his family. Wife has a job she really likes and aging parents who live nearby. Children's ties to area strong until they go off to college.
Fair compensation	Feels that reasonable compensation that he can count on for foreseeable future is more important than a higher salary that he cannot count on.
Compatible environment	Has found he is much happier and more successful working in an environment that's relatively harmonious.
Prefers marketing to sales	Has learned also that he's happier and more effective in a planning and support role than in a sales role.
Keep skills current	Has found his experience and skills in management and planning enable him to perform effectively and wants to keep those skills sharp by using them in next position.
Environment that minimizes weaknesses	Has developed ability to cope adequately (but not strongly) with two greatest weaknesses: dealing with aggressive confrontation and company politics.

ALTERNATIVE CAREER ANALYSIS

At the start of his search, Tom had identified some career alternatives. Let's review his thinking. Over the years he had worked closely with management consultants several times, and the consultants had recommended things his company had then implemented. Management consulting was an activity he thought he would enjoy and be good at, and he preferred it to line supervision. He liked the variety of things that consultants were exposed to, so he considered consulting as one possibility.

Several good friends had bought businesses with limited capital, planning to pay off their obligation by increasing the profits of the company. Several had been successful with companies they bought or started. Tom envied them because he visualized they were their own boss, they ran their own show, and they were apparently free from internal politics. He liked the idea of seeing whatever success he achieved accrue to him. He thought he could handle the hard work and the risk. Tom had run three large community activities, and his ideas and leadership brought good results. He got a lot of satisfaction from them. He felt he had the leadership skills to upgrade a business successfully if he could find an appropriate business to buy.

His other options were doing what he had done throughout his career, first as a marketing executive and then as a sales executive. He had filled several roles in both marketing and sales, so he understood what it took to be successful in both areas.

In the first six weeks of his search, Tom spent time researching these four alternatives: management consulting, buying a business, marketing, and sales. He talked with several people in each. He explained that he was looking for information, and most people were willing to help. They also gave him some valuable referrals to other people. It's important to speak not only with people who were successful in their fields, but also with people who were unsuccessful. Sometimes you learn much more from the people who had difficulties.

Tom saw the following people in this research stage:

◆ Two owners of large consulting firms
◆ Two owners of small consulting firms

- Two buyers of consulting services
- Three owners of small businesses
- Two owners of small businesses that had failed
- Two venture capitalists
- Two loan officers in a bank
- Two major customers of small businesses
- One supplier to small businesses
- Three top marketing executives
- Two successful sales managers
- Two professors in a business school

Tom asked them the following questions:

- What do you like about your job? What do you dislike?
- What do you do day to day, year to year?
- What does it take to succeed?
- Why do people fail?
- What are the greatest risks?
- How do I get into your field?
- How difficult is it to get into your field? What is the best way to go about it?
- What skills and temperament fit best?
- From what you know of me, how would you assess my chances of success?
- What do you see as the biggest obstacle I would have to face?
- What is the long-term earning potential?
- Who else might give me useful information?
- May I use your name when I call for an appointment?

Exhibit 3-7 • Alternative Careers Analysis for Tom Franks

Job Characteristic	My Goal	Management Consulting
Company stability	Avoid highly volatile struggling companies.	Little chance with established firm; unlikely to get good incom for several years, if ever.
Location	Avoid location change from current large city.	Won't have to move, may be lots of travel.
Fair compensation	Willing to trade off compensation for better stability.	Unlikely in early years, if ever; can continue beyond retirement
Compatible environment	Working with good people in non-tumultuous environment.	Should be reasonable, but isolated.
Prefers marketing to sales	Planning and supporting sales rather than just selling.	Much of success will depend or successful selling.
Keep skills current	In today's world, technology success based on staying current.	A key to being successful as consultant.
Minimizes weaknesses	To avoid having to deal with aggressive people, particularly in po-litically charged atmosphere.	Sales—not his strong point—is key to success.

Note: A refinement of this schedule is to assign a rating to each factor (say, my company's stability 20) and executive 15, etc. Then tally the grades to obtain a numerical total for each alternative career. Results should Tom Franks's alternative job analysis.

Before Tom analyzed his alternative careers, he updated his priorities list based on his current thinking. His revised set of priorities are shown under "My Goal" in Exhibit 3-7. He reduced the priority of "top salary" and "minimum search time" and increased the priority of "finding a comparatively low-risk job" and of "a compatible environment."

Marketing Executive	Buy My Own Business	Sales Executive
Most effective in this role; should have several choices with good search.	With limited capital, unlikely to find business with good prospects.	Uncomfortable and not very successful in this role; unlikely to get in strong company.
Shouldn't have to move.	Shouldn't have to move.	Shouldn't have to move.
Should be able to reach this goal.	Minimum in near term; possibly good after several years, but much capital at risk.	Possible highest compensation—large incentive factor.
Reasonable change. It will be good.	Should be reasonable.	Risky due to poor qualifications.
Will best use my experience and meet my interest.	Selling probably very important as well as making good product or providing useful service.	Success entirely based on successful selling.
Moderately important.	May or may not be important.	Moderately important.
Will be some, but probably at an acceptable level.	To sell successfully could be critical.	Probably quite a bit; may be a real stretch.

then grade each option on the factor. For example, management consulting might be 8, marketing be checked by gut feeling and several advisors' observations. This is demonstrated in Exhibit 3-8,

From his research Tom concluded that management consulting was unrealistic. Success in consulting would depend on something he was weak in: selling. He probably would not get a position with a well-established firm, so he would have to start consulting on his own. Realistically a consulting business would take three to five years to build up to generate an acceptable income, but he needed a good income immediately for his children's education. Finally, he decided he was temperamentally unsuited to the traveling, the ups and downs and pressures of consulting, and the difficult marketing in the early years.

Buying his own business was only a pipe dream, basically for similar reasons. Tom needed immediate income, and he was not willing to risk his limited capital. In addition, searching for a sound and suitable business to buy and financing it would undoubtedly take a long search.

He viewed a sales executive's job as similar to his Vice President of Marketing role in Fraser Software. Although his title was "Marketing Director," he had spent almost all his time selling. He had not done well, and he was unhappy. Therefore, a sales manager's job was a poor choice.

A marketing executive's job similar to Marketing Manager at Commercial Communications made the most sense. He wanted a job in a reasonably stable company with an apparently good working environment, and he was sure that several such jobs were available. Within his commuting range around Chicago, he guessed that there might be as many as 200 such jobs, although probably only a few were actually open. Given normal turnover and the constant need for marketing expertise, he was optimistic that he could find and be considered for several jobs within four to six months. Because the field was particularly open to unrecognized needs, he might be able to uncover several hidden jobs if he expanded his networking and did some blind prospecting. Because of the number of these marketing executive jobs, he thought he would probably find a couple of jobs that would be compatible with his skills and lifestyle.

Tom's career analysis is shown in Exhibit 3-7, "Alternative Careers Analysis." The insight Tom gained through this research was important. Now he actually understood the most appropriate line of work for himself. In addition, the time he spent in exploring career alternatives and conducting an intensive search helped him understand the job requirements for the type of marketing job he wanted. Several alternative careers and their pros and cons will be thoroughly discussed in Chapter 16, "Alternative Careers."

Again he contacted his trusted friend to review his career analysis.

ALTERNATIVE JOB ANALYSIS

The last step in this job search is to get one or more job offers that meet your priorities. The results of Tom's research when he was faced with a critical job choice is shown in Exhibit 3-8. Monarch Communications had not made him an offer, although he felt one might be close. This option was included in his analysis, however, because job hunters are frequently faced with the situation of "one or two birds in hand and maybe a better one in the bush." How to deal with this quandary is covered in Chapter 14, "Evaluating Offers and Making the Final Decision." At this decision point, review your thinking with a trusted friend. Tom did this and concluded his best strategy was to try to speed up an offer from Monarch. Several days later he received it substantially as he had estimated it, and he accepted it.

When he started out his search, Tom found he easily deluded himself by thinking of himself as he wanted to be, not as he actually was. As he talked with many people, however, he got a better idea of what really made him tick: his strengths, his weaknesses, his interests, his values, and his priorities. No one could determine for Tom which job to take—he had to decide that for himself.

Going through this process carefully and thoroughly clarified his "career values," which helped him make a good job choice. Several years later, he was approached with a good offer. He reappraised his priorities, which hadn't changed much. Furthermore, this thorough process of assessing priorities precluded his agonizing over his

Exhibit 3-8 • Alternative Job Analysis, Tom Franks

Job Characteristics	My Goal	Reliance Networks 75 Employees Marketing Director
Type business		Networking systems
Status of offer	Firm	Firm. Answer in 2 weeks
Job duties	Marketing	Development of marketing plan—sales off 8% in 2 yrs.
Company stability	Stable	Very volatile; going through major reorganization
Location	No move	No move likely
Risk	Low	Shaky past, uncertain future
Compensation	$100,000	$93,000 + 10% bonus; generous options (though now worthless)
Why available	_____	Predecessor fired; second in 3 years
Type of people	Prefer high-grade professionals	Known as tough people, didn't like two of five I met (including prospective boss)
Assessment of duties	_____	Very difficult job, hard to carry out to their expectations; question company's willingness to commit resources needed
Long-term prospects	Strong	Quite shaky
Base to move from	Strong	Questionable
Company's reputation	Good	Poor—several layoffs in last 2 years; lots of turnover
Traveling	Would prefer less than 10%	About 1/2 time
Pressure	Moderate	Very high

See grading procedure note on Exhibit 3-7.

ANV 310 Employees Technical Sales and Marketing Specialist	Monarch Communications 780 Employees Marketing Planning Specialist
Fiberoptics	Telecommunications
Firm. Answer in 3 weeks	Seems close
Mostly selling to big accounts, some planning	Running research and planning, backup to Director
Has been growing at 15% a year	Growing at 5% per year for past 4 years
Possible major move across U.S.	No move likely
Quite high, very competitive field	Lowest
$90,000 + 10-15% bonus	Guessing $90,000 + 5% bonus
New position	Predecessor retiring
Liked everyone pretty well, prospective boss ok	Excellent reputation; liked everyone I met, especially prospective boss
Taking over activity that's been VP's baby; seems like real opportunity to make my mark	Looks like things running fairly smoothly; would expect good support
Think there's a good chance of my success; feel less optimistic about company's prospects	Company's prospects probably good for 5 years, expect major change in industry then
Pretty good	Pretty good
Good—seems behind times, moderate layoffs and turnover	Excellent, no layoffs, low turnover
About 1/5 of time	Practically none
Quite high	Moderate

choice after the fact. He had worked through the process thoroughly, and had made a careful and justified choice at the time. He turned down the offer.

Your best guarantee of making a sound decision is to go through the tedious, hard work that Tom did. If you go about this process aggressively, you can likely evaluate alternative careers effectively in four to six weeks. The process makes you a more effective job hunter, so it will likely speed up your finding a suitable job and improve your chances of making a good choice.

CHAPTER 4

THE JOB SEARCH FROM THE EMPLOYER'S SIDE OF THE DESK

ACKNOWLEDGING THE EMPLOYERS' PROBLEMS

When you are job hunting, remember that you must win the favor of one or more employers. You must make them feel and believe you are the safest and best person they can hire. To do that, you need to focus on how employers evaluate candidates.

Many job hunters feel that "good jobs are hard to find." Many employers, however, feel that "good people are hard to find." It often takes employers two months, sometimes six months or more, to fill key jobs, particularly when unemployment is low and there's strong competition in the hiring market for people with good skills. Companies and recruiters can accelerate the recruiting process considerably by using the Internet, scanners, and computer screening to accumulate a much larger pool of candidates than before. Electronic transmission and storage of most marketable resumes enables employers to process high numbers of applicants by storing the applications directly in their database. At job fairs employers are often deluged with candidates, but few are the kind of candidate that the employer is seeking: job hunters with the strong specialized skills that the employer needs.

A surprisingly large number of jobs advertised in such places as the *Wall Street Journal*, the *New York Times*, and the *National Ad Search Weekly* are unfilled after three or four months, in spite of the fact that there are quite a few qualified candidates. Locating candidates, evaluating them through their resumes and then through interviews, getting the necessary people to agree on the hiring decision, and negotiating the compensation package can be complex and slow. Good people *can be* hard to find!

Problems commonly arise when job hunters look at the job from their standpoint, not the employer's standpoint. Mary Friedman, Executive Vice President of Temple Technology was dissatisfied with Temple's information technology and networking operations. In the process of trying to straighten out some operational problems in that department, eventually she fired her Director of Information Technology because of the delays and confusion in implementing the needed changes. After six weeks' of aggressive recruiting by Human Resources, Mary had seen only two candidates—both weak ones. One day she stormed into the office of Sally Harrington, the Director of Human Resources, and asked her what was taking so long. Harrington said she had over 200 resumes and that she had selected what she thought were the best two for interviews, but Mary was welcome to review the resumes herself. As Mary left Sally's office with the resumes, Sally said, "I'll bet you'll be in here tomorrow, having reached the same conclusion." Sure enough, that's what happened. Mary and Sally concluded that some of the candidates probably were qualified, but their resumes emphasized improving the software and expanding the operation, not straightening out operational problems, which was Mary's first priority. When Mary met her peers from other companies and discussed IT operations, most of them were equally frustrated in trying to get better coordination and control of them.

This is a classic case of the job applicants' being so focused on their goals that they didn't pay any attention to the employer's needs. The successful candidate very quickly sized up Mary's needs and convincingly explained his experience in straightening out a similarly fouled up IT operation.

Some job hunters have difficulty because their concept of the job they're seeking is too narrow. Their search is colored by their experience with their former company and their former boss's view of the job. Working for the same company for a long time can lead to this problem. A narrow concept of the job you are seeking may prompt you to overlook suitable opportunities or target your resumes to a job description that is too narrow. Avoid this by designing your resume to show that you have a wide variety of skills in your field. In Chapter 6, "Making Your Resume an Effective Tool," you'll see how to organize your credentials so that they appear most favorable for the type of job you're seeking.

Hiring Managers are also influenced by their past experiences. If the prior job holder performed badly, the Hiring Manager will be drawn to candidates who appear strong in the areas in which the prior employee was weak. In addition, job candidates are often screened extensively and carefully but then fail on the job. Sometimes a new hire is dissatisfied with the job and leaves, often abruptly. These failures can take place within 12 months. So, although there are lots of candidates, there may be only a few that fit the profile the Hiring Manager wants.

UNDERSTANDING THE DIFFICULTIES IN RECRUITING

Employers have recruiting difficulties because they have high standards and because the hiring process is complicated. Most companies find that the best way to fill a position is to assemble a large pool of candidates and evaluate their resumes first by computer or manually, then by telephone interviews, and then by a series of personal interviews with a senior Human Resources person and finally the Hiring Manager and a few of his or her associates. Unfortunately, individual prejudices and poor judgment can get in the way. It takes a lot of skill to identify the best candidate. To help you in your job search, look at yourself as a candidate from an employer's perspective by reviewing some of the recruitments you or your associates have made in the past:

+ Why were some recruitments successful? Why did others fail?

+ How did certain candidates impress you? What characteristics seemed favorable and unfavorable?

+ How did others turn you off? Some of the bad impressions may have been due to errors in your judgment or problems in your recruiting practices. Or you may have been using an unrealistic or vague job description, an inadequate pool of candidates, or the prejudices of your associates. Some of the bad impressions were no doubt due to the ineffective way the candidates presented themselves; they may have been too self-oriented or inadequately prepared, or they may have emphasized experience irrelevant to your needs. Understanding what makes a good impression or a bad impression on an employer may help you present yourself more effectively.

An employer selects a final candidate based on three criteria:

+ Does the candidate have strong (though not necessarily the best) relevant qualifications and skills?

+ Is the candidate likely to fit in with the boss and the organization? "Is this person one of us?" This is the "clubability factor." Anyone hired is joining a club, so candidates are evaluated on their compatibility with other club members, as well as on their experience.

- Does the applicant appear to have the aura, personality, and motivation to solve the job's most important current problems? Does he or she also appear able to adapt effectively to changed conditions, such as a change in the economy?

Evaluating Your Technical Abilities

Strong pertinent knowledge is crucial to any job. In preparing your resume, remember that increasingly employers are using computerized scanners to profile and screen candidates for many jobs, particularly technical ones. They search for indications of technical capabilities, such as numbers and technical terms. If you're looking for a technical job, design your resume so it's in line with a Hiring Manager's likely preferences. To do that, evaluate your technical qualifications as a Hiring Manager would:

- Are your technical qualifications up to date?
- Are you skilled in the technical requirements needed one year from now? Are you the type that's also likely to be current three years from now?
- Do you present your technical qualifications effectively to semi-technical people such as recruiters and hiring managers?
- Do you present your qualifications effectively to technical people, such as senior scientists and engineers?
- Are you likely to be accepted personally by the technical people?

Evaluating Your Personal Characteristics

Personal characteristics are so important that they often elevate one candidate among several with equivalent technical skills. Personal characteristics sought after are the ability to think under pressure, enthusiasm, flexibility, the ability to lead, and growth potential. Your universal skills, elicited by the questions listed below, apply to all jobs regardless of level and type. Undoubtedly, a prospective employer will evaluate you on some of them:

+ Would you get projects done on time, within budget?

+ Are you likely to be resourceful? Will you find solutions to critical problems when others don't?

+ Will helping your boss accomplish his or her goals be a top priority?

+ Would you expect and forestall problems, rather than just react to them?

+ Is keeping your boss well informed without wasting his or her valuable time one of your priorities?

+ Do you communicate well?

+ Are you likely to be loyal?

+ Are you likely to hit the ground running?

+ Are you likely to come up with useful ideas?

+ Would you perform well on a high-priority task for which you were the best person available at the time, even though your credentials for it are weak?

+ Will you work well without close supervision?

+ How long are you likely to stay?

+ Would you follow through?

+ Would you do the nitty gritty tasks (a key to success in most jobs) as well as the glamorous projects?

+ Would you set priorities and achieve them?

+ Are you likely to be effective in developing other people's skills and talents?

+ Are you adaptable to considerably different situations should conditions change?

* Would you be credible?
* Would you be well informed and motivated to learn?
* Would you work well under pressure?

So be prepared to describe an experience that exemplifies each characteristic. In an actual interview, you would probably ask what three or four characteristics the Hiring Manager considered most important. You would then give him or her an example of experiences you've had when those characteristics were pivotal to your success.

Writing the Job Description

List the principal functions and personal characteristics mentioned most frequently in ads in the *Wall Street Journal*, the *New York Times*, and your nearest metropolitan daily newspaper as well as on the Internet. Also survey Nationaladsearch.com (site of the *National Ad Search Weekly*), which is a compilation of ads from various sources across the country, company Web sites, and online career sites. Newspaper ads are fewer now than five years ago, but some of them have more information than they used to. They can help you identify what recruiters are looking for in candidates for the job you're seeking. Exhibit 4-1 is an informative ad. An ad with such detail can be very useful in designing a target letter or in preparing for an interview.

Now prepare a job description listing the principal functions and personal characteristics you've identified. It's important that your description reflect current needs rather than those of a different economy of several years ago. Emphasize these characteristics in your resume and in interviews. Also look for any functional experience you lack. Part of your preparation is to develop a strategy to cope with such deficiencies (see Chapter 11, "Preparing for Interviews.")

The main reasons that people fail at a certain job will be paramount in the minds of employers. If you want to be a sales manager, think about why sales managers fail. Perhaps sales managers don't

Exhibit 4-1 • An Informative Ad

Chief Technical Officer (CTO)
Alter Technologies, Inc.

The CTO will define Alter's path to the future and articulate its future vision. The CTO will be responsible for defining and implementing the overall technology strategy for the company. The CTO's focus will be to place Alter in a position of competitive advantage and to seek ways to extend, expand, and differentiate its leading-edge technology. The CTO reports directly to the CEO and collaborates closely with the executive team, Board of Directors, and R&D teams.

Experience should include 10+ years in positions of technology leadership and a proven ability to take theoretical approaches to create market-driven and profitable business solutions. Must have knowledge of broad spectrum of advanced technologies, including some of the following: advanced modeling, software architecture and design, optimization, evolutionary and adaptive technologies, data analytics, neural networks, and high-volume data transmission, manipulation, retrieval, and storage techniques.

Must be familiar with intellectual property protection and have the ability to foster innovation to expand the company's already superior patent portfolio. Position requires superior communication skills, including translation of complex technical concepts. Record of attracting and retaining strong technical talent and inspiring confidence in internal and external constituencies a must. Masters/Ph.D. in engineering or science with solid mathematics underpinning necessary.

The ideal candidate will receive an excellent compensation and benefits plan, including a competitive base salary, significant bonus opportunities, incentive stock options, and relocation assistance. (No agencies or phone calls, please.) Respond in confidence to Dept. A, Alter Technologies, USA.

---

meet their company's sales goals or expense targets, or they don't push new products, or they don't reorganize poorly performing territories. Beware of these failures, and be prepared to demonstrate to the interviewer your experience in coping with these problems.

To get a better perspective on the market for your skills, write a realistic and specific description of the job you're seeking. The general job description found in most manuals isn't good enough. You'll need one that outlines the principal functions of the job in depth (the important items that are critical to an employer). List the six to eight functional items that you think an employer is most likely to be looking for. Then prioritize them. Next prepare a job description for the

EXHIBIT 4-2 • Job Description for a Sales Manager

Education	MBA
Experience	10–15 years in sales and sales management
Personal characteristics	Persuasive, aggressive, flexible, outgoing, innovative, and competitive
Working conditions	High pressure; constantly working under hard-to-make and easy-to-measure targets; lots of travel, lots of entertaining
Long-range possibilities	Good opportunity to move into top management (often to Vice President of Sales with the right administrative skills)
Pros	Challenging, exciting, high compensation (based more on job success than in most fields), great opportunity to make a mark
Cons	Continual pressure, demanding on personal life, high risk
	Functional experience needed (in decreasing order of importance):
	Increasing sales
	Decreasing expenses
	Improving profit margins
	Building an effective sales force
	Introducing new products
	Developing new markets
	Improving distribution methods
	Reducing field inventory

job you're seeking, such as shown in Exhibit 4-2, "Job Description for a Sales Manager."

Once you have identified the key attributes that the employer may be looking for in filling the job you are seeking, you are ready to examine your experience, with the goal of presenting it most effectively.

CHAPTER 5

IMPROVING YOUR ATTRACTIVENESS TO EMPLOYERS

PRESENTING YOURSELF FAVORABLY

Many people believe that job hunters overstate their qualifications. In fact, some do, but many job hunters understate some, overlook a few, and present others ineffectively. Your most important task is to *prepare to present yourself most favorably to everyone you deal with in your job search*. Presenting yourself as favorably as possible is critical because you usually have only one chance to clear each of the hurdles leading to an offer. What's more, all employers will regard each of your actions as your best. So being at your best is important.

Presenting yourself favorably requires using accomplishment statements to describe your experience. You should use them in every aspect of your search, such as in networking, dealing with recruiters, making appointments, and interviewing. Accomplishments are "the language of job hunting."

Now, let's look at remembering your achievements, organizing them, and presenting them most favorably.

REMEMBERING ALL YOUR ACCOMPLISHMENTS

Sam Carbone was an experienced executive in his late forties who had lost his job as Assistant Chief Engineer of Maverick Ltd. due to a management change. One day Sam had a particularly discouraging interview with Champion Machine for a job that really excited him and for which he felt well qualified. He was sure he had botched the interview. That evening, as he was getting his thoughts together for an interview with Arrow Products the next day, his frustration turned into indignation and he blurted out, "I know damn well I'm very qualified for that Champion job. After all, I straightened out the development engineering problems on the Arrowhead line that everyone else had given up on, and it became one of Maverick's most profitable lines. I also reengineered the Temple line when it was failing, and it became one of the company's most important lines." Sam realized he hadn't mentioned the Arrowhead accomplishment during his interview and had presented the Temple experience ineffectively. His outburst was a valuable way of expanding his thinking. Nurturing your frustrations can help jog your memory.

Sam then remembered two other accomplishments he hadn't included in his resume or in any of his eight interviews to date. He had mentioned two other accomplishments only briefly in a couple of interviews because he assumed the employers would automatically understand their full implications. From the employers' bland reactions, apparently they didn't.

In addition, Sam had completely overlooked an important community activity: his membership on the building committee for a major addition to his church. He gained valuable experience in dealing with an architect and in overseeing construction. He persuaded the committee to select a relatively unknown architect—a successful choice. These skills helped prepare him for his next job as a division general manager. Overlooking key accomplishments is a frequent way job hunters undersell themselves.

RECOGNIZING YOUR MAJOR ACCOMPLISHMENTS

Make a comprehensive list of the most significant accomplishments of your career, using *career* in its broadest sense. Start with college, both your academic and extracurricular activities and summer jobs. Include summer jobs, each regular job, and community activities. From this list, select 15 to 25 of your most notable achievements. Let's look at some ways to do this.

For each of your jobs and community activities, list all of your responsibilities and your accomplishments. Include even minor accomplishments at this stage. For an example, see Exhibit 5-1, "Job Accomplishments Chart."

EXHIBIT 5-1 • Job Accomplishments Chart

Dates	Company	Title	Responsibility	Accomplishments
8/98–6/01	MNO	Buyer	Reducing purchase prices	Changed competitive bidding system
				Concentrated on large volume items
				Used maxim castings
			Coping with short supply	Rescheduled Magna stainless steel
			Developing new sources	Signed General Rubber for Foxcroft housings
6/01–4/03	Peerless Machinery	Assistant purchasing agent	Managing department	Reorganized administration plan
				Met weekly with buyers
			Subcontracting	Revised program Developed new contract
			Reporting	Computerized the daily shortage report
				Recorded variation from plan weekly

Accomplishments typically result from the following activities:

- Reducing costs by introducing procedures, improving work flow, or decreasing overhead
- Increasing sales by opening up new markets, getting existing customers to buy additional or new products, improving customer relations
- Improving quality by decreasing rejects or getting suppliers to improve their products
- Using assets better by increasing inventory and turnover, improving collections
- Motivating employees by improving incentive systems, communicating better
- Improving productivity by improving training, upgrading recruitment, offering better incentives
- Introducing technology by upgrading computer systems, improving machine tools

Looking at the changes that affected each job helps you remember the things you did on that job. For each of these changes, ask yourself what changes occurred in your work and what your resulting accomplishments were. For example, four years ago Jane Foster became the Purchasing Agent. Several months later Bill Smith was moved over from Buyer of Raw Materials to Buyer of Subcontract Assemblies. A few months after that, Bill was asked to be department coordinator on the new quality control system. Jane's appointment was a key change for Bill, leading to these two changes in his duties.

Recalling the principal people you worked with on every job or special assignment may also jog your memory. Some of these people may help you identify significant company accomplishments you were involved in.

Another way to recall accomplishments is to answer the following questions:

* What promotions have you had?
* What compliments were you paid on any aspect of your work?
* What merit salary increases have you had?
* What added responsibilities did you get?
* What extra committee assignments did you get?
* What other leadership roles have you assumed on the job or in the community?
* What special projects did you do?
* Under what circumstances were you asked to represent your organization?
* In what situations have you excelled over your peers?

Also scan your files, work diaries, and expense books to jog your memory.

Don't shortchange yourself on these exercises because they are key to your job search. Make the most exhaustive list of your accomplishments that you can. You probably won't be able to remember them all at one sitting, so keep a notebook handy for writing down others as you remember them. You'll recall accomplishments—at odd times: when you're driving, watching TV, shopping, and sometimes in the middle of the night. This is a time to "toot your own horn."

Select 15 to 25 of the accomplishments that are most marketable for the job you're seeking. Focus on what employers look for in hiring for your target job (see Chapter 4, "The Job Search from the Employer's Side of the Desk"). Select other accomplishments that may make a favorable impression in your resume—to show positive personal characteristics and specific skills.

A single achievement may exemplify several skills and personal characteristics. For example, you may have prepared a report that changed an important operating procedure, an important change that was resisted. Such a report shows your skills in being creative, analyzing, persuading, persevering, working under pressure, being accepted by various people, meeting deadlines, and implementing your ideas.

A single accomplishment also may show different skills at different stages of a project. For example, in revising a computer system, you may have been involved in all phases or only one phase: in analyzing the old system, designing the new one, implementing it, and using it or expanding it or refining it. Each phase may show different skills.

PRESENTING YOUR ACCOMPLISHMENTS

Mary Oxford was a lawyer who left her big, inner-city firm to move to the suburbs to raise a family. There she joined a firm where she did mostly routine real estate transactions with an occasional special project. On her original resume, buried in the detail was the statement, "Did the legal work for a 100-boat marina." When questioned, here's how she described this project:

- Was asked by the owner to be the project manager for the construction of a $3.5 million dollar marina for 100 boat slips with indoor rack storage for 110 boats
- Was in charge of an eight-person team: an architect, a surveyor, a structural engineer, an environmental consultant, and the contractors
- Oversaw designing the facilities, estimating the costs, and putting the project out for bid
- Successfully applied for 15 local, state, and federal permits; made a presentation on the project at the numerous public hearings
- Obtained approval from the local planning board, building board, and conservation committee

- Coordinated the construction phase, including the demolition, hazardous waste cleanup, dredging, and construction of the building, the million dollar seawall, and the marina

Obviously this project entailed more than the single item she had described in her original resume. When she revised her resume to fully describe this marina project and a similar one, she got more and better interviews.

PARs

You too must present your accomplishments most effectively. To help you, there's an easy formula called *PAR*. For each of your accomplishments, answer the following three questions:

- What was the Problem?
- What Action did you take?
- What was the Result?

For each of your principal accomplishments, write a PAR analysis. A PAR not only describes the responsibility you had but also your skill in handling it. Rough notes are OK (see Exhibit 5-2). This exercise helps you develop a bulleted item for your resume and material for cover letters, phone conversations, networking, and job interviews. Keep your PAR worksheets for future reference because you may want to revisit this exercise.

Word your PARs to convey the salient aspects of your accomplishment. Here's an example: "Since 1998, increased sales 40 percent (sales up $14 million). Increased profits $3.1 million in 2000, when I became Vice President." Note the three distinct accomplishments in one PAR:

- Increased sales
- Increased profits
- Promoted to Vice President

EXHIBIT 5-2 • A PAR Write-Up

Problem	Field salespeople were deluged with new products. Thus, they hadn't made much effort to sell them. Sales management and Product Development were very upset.
Action	Designed a sales training program emphasizing sales of new products.
	Arranged and conducted a kickoff sales meeting—emphasizing new products.
	Also arranged to have new products discussed at quarterly sales meetings.
	Got new product sales separately identified in monthly reports.
	Got sales force to report customer problems with these products.
Result	In past year, new products increased from 1.8 to 10.2% of total sales.
Resume bullet	Designed and implemented a sales training program for new products that increased their sales from 1.8 to 10.2% of total sales.
The skills used in this accomplishment	Analyzed problem.
	Conceived new program.
	Convinced sales management to implement program.
	Designed and conducted meetings.
	Arranged for reporting program.
	Followed up to see that all aspects of the program worked properly.

Here are some pointers for developing your PARs into resume bulleted items:

♦ Start each item with an action word (see the examples, page 65).

♦ Use simple, understandable language with few technical terms.

♦ Try to keep each item to two lines or less.

♦ Describe obstacles you overcame.

♦ Quantify your accomplishments (cost savings, increases in sales, quality, efficiency using dollars, percentages, etc.):

  • *Poor:* Recruited and trained 300 people

- *Better:* In a tight market, recruited over 300 technical people.
  Developed training programs to upgrade rapidly
  needed skills.
  Achieved lowest turnover in our industry.
- When you can't recall the numbers, estimate conservatively.
  Stretching to get the largest number is less important than the skills
  you demonstrate in organizing the project and completing it.
- When you were a member of a group that accomplished some-
  thing, say "Played a key role in."
- Focus on accomplishments of the last five years.
- In an interview, be prepared to elaborate, describing the skills or
  personal qualities involved in each PAR, such as being hard-
  working, being a team player, getting others to work with you,
  being a leader, being creative, and being bottom-line oriented.
- Describe accomplishments in your PARs, not responsibilities:
  - *Poor (a responsibility):* Was responsible for overseeing a
    TQM program.
  - *Better (an accomplishment):* Oversaw the operation of a TQM
    program that reduced scrap from 6 to 2 percent.
- If your principal accomplishments are few but very involved, describe each one in considerable detail. (See the marina example
  just described.)

Sometimes you feel strongly that a particular accomplishment is
important, but you don't know how to express it. Writing down a PAR
about it often helps you see a way to present it effectively.

For example, Sam Ferguson's early experience was in operations,
but after five years he realized he was more interested in and better
suited to finance. He was able to make this change in a lateral move,
but his lack of accounting was a great disadvantage. He enrolled in
an intensive CPA Review program, skipping the prerequisite accounting courses. Within a year, he had passed the CPA exam, being

one of the 4 percent in the state who passed all four sections of it at one time. His PAR read, "Was one of 4 percent who passed all four sections of the state CPA exam at one time, with only accounting education being an intensive night CPA review course." This accomplishment helped him get his two subsequent senior financial positions. One Hiring Manager reacted to that PAR by saying, "That shows you're really smart and highly motivated."

Sometimes an important accomplishment doesn't seem relevant for the type of job you're seeking. Develop your PAR anyway. Although it may not be suitable for your resume, you may be able to use it effectively in an interview.

Occasionally you can't quantify an accomplishment. Nevertheless, describe it as effectively as you can. For example, "Convinced Illinois Appeals Court to revise its definition of agriculture in zoning cases."

Exhibit 5-3 shows various ways the PAR technique can be used. You'll find a much greater variety of PAR examples in *Best Resumes for $100,000+ Jobs* by Wendy S. Enelow, Impact Publications, 2001.

Once you've completed your list of PARs, ask a trusted friend to review them with you—perhaps a workshop associate. Tell him or her you'd like to review, say, three of the most important ones. Describe each accomplishment. Ask him or her to interrupt for any needed clarifications. Then each of you write down your version of the PAR for comparison and to develop a strong statement. This exercise will often sharpen up the PAR. After you've done three or four in depth, you should be able to improve the rest of them yourself. If in several interviews, one or several aren't having the impact you think they deserve, review them in the same way.

Using PARs

Your PARs provide you with the basic material you need to present yourself effectively throughout your job search: in resumes, in cover

EXHIBIT 5-3 • PAR Examples

- Developed a coating process to delay the corrosion of tanks that deferred for over 5 years the replacement of tanks that would have cost $725,000.

- Identified additional foreign income, allowing an increase of $3.7 million in foreign credit utilization.

- Redesigned external brackets from castings to forgings, reducing product cost 7% and considerably improving quality.

- Built new relationships in the Cincinnati and Dayton areas, generating increased loan balances of $90 million and deposits of $8 million.

- Achieved the lowest accident rate of the four plants of the Assembly Division, for 4 consecutive years. Our plant was awarded the highest safety award of the Midwest Manufacturers Association.

- Developed and conducted an attitude survey that led to improved supervision and raised low morale, reducing shift absenteeism from 17 to 6%.

- Created and conducted an interviewer training program for managers and supervisors that reduced candidate selection ratio from 1 out of 13 to 1 out of 4.

- Reduced receivables from 57 to 33 days.

- Redesigned tools distributor sales network, which realized a sales increase of 234% to $1.7 million.

- Initiated an absenteeism control program for 275 salaried employees that reduced overall absences 57%.

- Conducted a study of the purchase and distribution of legal forms to branch locations in the U.S. that resulted in a new forms inventory system for our 237 branches that saved $350,000.

- Coordinated five state agencies and outside counsel in defense and satisfactory settlement of an $11 million lawsuit brought by Allied Steel Co.

letters, on the phone, in dealing with recruiters, in networking, and in interviews.

In your resume, use your PARs as is, as bulleted items.

In cover letters, in many cases use them also as is. However, you may want to shorten some.

In dealing with recruiters, in networking and in job interviews, lengthen the PAR statement to a two-minute description so the interviewer understands the problems you faced, the actions you took, and your style of carrying them out.

On the phone, when you're blind prospecting, use PARs as is, in the bulleted form.

Marty Feinberg had related one of his most important PARs numerous times, yet it had always been met with a bland response, which exasperated him. In preparing for an important job interview, he realized he had assumed that interviewers would understand what a great achievement he was talking about. Apparently they had not. This time, he spelled it out in much more detail, and he got a good response: "That shows you've got the kind of drive we like around here."

If you feel you're not coming across as well as you should, *experiment* with your presentation, especially in networking interviews, which are low risk.

Expanded PARs

PARs are the principal way you communicate your experience through your accomplishments. You may find it necessary to expand them to demonstrate the skills involved:

PAR: Developed and conducted an attitude survey that led to improved supervision and overcame low morale, reducing shift absenteeism from 17 to 6 percent.

Expanded PAR: At a time when our main plant of 1600 was working a lot of overtime, morale had deteriorated and absenteeism had increased to 17 percent. Initiated the idea of an attitude survey, which was approved by the operations committee. The results of the survey of all blue- and white-collar employees showed a wide variety of complaints and the feeling that management was generally unresponsive to them. Developed and conducted a training program for first-line supervisors so that within several months, there was marked improvement in morale and absenteeism dropped to 6 percent.

A strong list of PARs is excellent preparation for writing a winning resume.

CHAPTER 6

MAKING YOUR RESUME AN EFFECTIVE TOOL

PERSPECTIVE

A good resume is one of the key tools you use in your job search. You'll use it primarily in three ways:

1. To notify a lot of people that you're looking for a job and to summarize your experience

2. To state that you have strong qualifications for the kind of job you're seeking

3. To sharpen your thinking about the experiences that make you a strong candidate

Writing a good resume will help you present yourself effectively in all activities of your search. A resume should be geared to the needs of the person reading it. For example, an employer looks at an unsolicited resume with two questions in mind:

1. Do I need anyone with this background?

2. Is the person's background strong enough to make an interview worthwhile?

Most employers look at a resume, particularly an unsolicited one, for 15 to 30 seconds to decide whether they want to read it more carefully. If they do read further, they're looking for answers to the following questions:

- Does this person have experience we currently need?
- How successful has this person been in the past?
- Is this person likely to be successful here?
- Will this person fit in well and perform effectively in our organization?

Think of your resume as an advertisement: You're advertising yourself for a job. Ads are concise to get attention quickly, they emphasize what the reader is interested in, and they have enough information to encourage the reader's interest and prompt the next step. In your job search, the next step is getting an interview.

TYPES OF RESUMES

There are four principal types of resumes: chronological, networking, functional, and Internet. The *chronological resume* lists your experience in reverse chronological order (most recent experience first) (see Exhibit 6-1, Herbert Gleason.) A *networking resume* is one page long and provides a way for the reader to get a quick picture of your experiences (see Exhibit 6-2, Fred Barkley.) A *functional resume* lists your experience by general types of activity (broad functional areas) with your job history at the end (see Exhibit 6-3, Karen Cox). An Internet resume is designed to be scored favorably in computerized screening, which gives highest grades to those that are filled with numbers, acronyms, and key word phrases (see Exhibit 6-4, Betsy Percival).

A chronological resume is preferable for most job seekers, but a functional resume may be appropriate if you're changing careers, have a gap in your work history (such as making a career change or are a homemaker returning to the job market), have had weak recent experiences, or have changed jobs frequently. The "Troubleshooting" section at the end of this chapter describes several people with unusual backgrounds who found they did best with a specially designed resume that presented themselves most effectively.

Both chronological and functional resumes can be deliberately designed as scannable resumes, which are required to apply for jobs on the Internet or at large companies that get many applicants for technical and/or lower-level jobs. In scanning, the resumes are read and graded by computer, a process that takes as little as three seconds per resume. Sometimes the resume is automatically transposed into the recruiter's own format for easy evaluation. Those scored highest by the computer are then screened by hand. The use of scanning is expanding rapidly because it allows recruiters to screen large pools of candidates quickly. Resumes with many numbers, acronyms, short phrases, and technical terms have the best chance of being scanned favorably.

Recruiting via the Internet generates the highest number of candidates. Because scanning and screening by the computer is so technical, this type of recruiting is changing rapidly. More and more recruiters and companies expect resumes to be sent by e-mail, so in your networking with recent or current job hunters, ask for criticism of your Internet resume and advice on submitting it by e-mail to executive and company recruiters and in answering ads, as well as to the Internet recruiters. Collect samples of good Internet resumes you run across to help you prepare a good one.

FEATURES OF RESUMES

Write your own resume; don't have somebody else do it. Writing a resume makes you think through and organize your experience, a process that helps you make a favorable impression in all the activities of your job search.

Remember what employers are looking for in the ideal candidate. Your work in developing your job description is useful here (see Exhibit 4-2, "Job Description for a Sales Manager").

EXHIBIT 6-1 • A Two-Page Chronological Resume.
Chronological resumes are the most commonly used type of resume, and they are very much preferred by most executive and company recruiters.

HERBERT L. GLEASON

223 Somerville Road
Ottawa, WA 98111
206-783-9211
E-Mail: herb_gleason@aol.com

(a) MBA Finance & Marketing
University of Washington
BS General Engineering
Washington State University

(b)**SUMMARY**

Experienced financial manager with a solid track record of accomplishments in large and small companies; 18 years with Garrison Equipment in manufacturing and division offices. Areas of strength include:

- Strategic planning
- Budgeting and analysis
- Cost accounting and controls

- Cash management
- Financial reporting
- Information systems implementation

EXPERIENCE

BURNHAM & HANKS CONSULTING, SEATTLE, WA
(c)*A publicly traded 120-person computers and software applications consulting service firm*

1997–   **Chief Financial Officer**
Brought into company to upgrade and strengthen financial and administrative functions as part of expansion into turnkey water supply business. Shortly afterward, a recession and delays in initial turnkey projects forced company to retrench to consulting.

(d)• Shored up deteriorating financial condition through sale/leaseback of assets, renegotiation of bank loans, private placement of additional equity and aggressive cash management, reducing receivables from 70 to 40 days.

• Established budgeting procedures and business controls in marketing and project management, cutting costs and reducing markdowns 40%.

• Renegotiated $3 million international contract with US government agency to provide adequate profit margin and simpler reporting.

• Completely restructured accounting and computer systems procedures, cutting time needed to prepare financial statements from 8+ to 4 days; decreased auditing costs over 50%.

• Brought all SEC and shareholder reporting in-house, meeting all deadlines with savings of professional fees of over $35,000.

• Initiated review of employee health insurance program that decreased annual growth in premiums from 11 to 4%.

(a) Placement of your strong education here draws immediate attention to it, without detracting attention from the summary and your most recent experience.

(b) There is no objective because the summary serves as one. Many prefer to also have an objective, which in this case would be management or financial executive

(c) If the company is not well known, you should include a brief description of it.

(d) A key to a resume's effectiveness is using your PARs to describe your experience.

Herbert L. Gleason, page 2

GARRISON EQUIPMENT CORP., CHICAGO, IL   CORPORATE OFFICES
A 48,000-employee manufacturer of computers, electronic products and systems

1993–1997   **Performance Measurement Program Manager**
Reported to corporate controller, worked closely with senior management, directed a major overhaul of product line accounting, intracompany pricing and quota setting in anticipation of organizational changes associated with conversion to RISC technology.

• Built and led a team from finance, systems, and sales administration that completed program in required 12 months, providing supplemental performance reporting in new format prior to annual budget cycle.

1988–1993   **Financial Reporting Software Division Manager**
Managed the support and development of financial reporting software used worldwide by 150 entities for external and management reporting.

• Headed a $5 million project creating a decentralized system for integrated management and external reporting.

• Recruited top-notch staff (5 of 7 of whom became division controllers).

• Shortened overall reporting cycle from 9 to 3 days while expanding coverage to include international installations, sales force, and service organizations.

GARRISON EQUIPMENT CORP., CHICAGO, IL   DATA SYSTEMS DIVISION
Major division with $100+ million annual sales minicomputer and systems business; 700 employees

1983–1988   **Cost Accounting Manager—General Accounting Manager**
Managed all divisional accounting functions and related systems activities. Supported division management team in business planning, budgeting, and performance reviews.

• Developed method for predicting impact of design changes on manufacturing overhead to ensure accurate cost projections for new product pricing.

• Improved department efficiency keeping staff growth considerably below revenue growth.

PREVIOUS EXPERIENCE

1980–1983   **Financial Analyst:** Responsible for worldwide product line financial planning, reporting, and consolidation; pricing reviews; business modeling; and special projects.

(e)
PROFESSIONAL AND CIVIC AFFILIATIONS

Financial Executive Institute of Chicago, President, 1993–1994
United Way, Hinsdale, IL, Campaign Chairman, 1989–1990

(e) An expanded education section can be included here, though it's not necessary.

EXHIBIT 6-2 • A One-Page Resume

The resume below can be particularly useful in networking.

FRED BARKLEY

23 Emmons Drive   **920-705-3683**
Appleton, WI 54911   **FredBarkley@aol.com**

OBJECTIVE	General or Manufacturing Management
CREDENTIALS	17 years of experience managing domestic and international operations including direct P&L responsibility for a $20 million division.
	Solid experience in manufacturing, finance, and sales.
	Known for leadership, managerial, and organizational skills in startup and turn-around situations.
	Proven ability to reduce waste in all areas and to manage assets, and known as a capable negotiator.
	Have studied and worked with Dr. W. Edwards Deming in quality improvement and waste reduction.
	Lived in Mexico 4 years, fluent in Spanish.

MAJOR
ACHIEVEMENTS

- Directed foreign subsidiaries whose sales increased 75% to $130 million while profits grew 87% to $15 million.

- Planned and directed the startup of two foreign assembly plants, sourcing locally 90% of the parts. Initial capital $3.0 million.

- Launched two new products which achieved sales of over $30 million within 2 years.

- Directed the purchase versus manufacture of an existing $20 million product line changing it from a 5% loss to a profit of 11%.

- In most recent assignment, reduced waste $600,000, WIP inventory $30,000,000, quality returns $195,000, and raw material costs $800,000.

EXPERIENCE   ACME CORPORATION 1983–Present   APPLETON, WI
A $650 million specialty paper manufacturer

Assistant General Manager	1998-
Director, Subsidiary Operations	1994-1998
Director, Manufacturing and Procurement	1991-1994
General Manager, Mexico City	1988-1991
Plant Manager, Mexico City	1987-1988
Plant Production Manager	1985-1987
Assistant to Plant Manager	1983-1985

EDUCATION   Accounting and Economics, BBA, 1983, New York University
Strategic Marketing Program, Stanford University

EXHIBIT 6-3 • A Functional Resume

A functional type of resume tends to be frowned on by executive, company, and Internet recruiters because they're suspicious it's being used to cover up weaknesses. On the other hand, it can be effective for certain situations as in career changes, long successful careers prior to poor recent experiences, and frequent job changes. It's more likely to be effective in networking and blind prospecting.

KAREN COX

35 Decatur Road	University of Pittsburgh, MBA Honors
Atlanta, GA 30321	Houston University, BS Honors
404-687-9321	Electrical Engineering
Karen_Cox@aol.com	

OBJECTIVE Senior Position in Manufacturing Management.

CREDENTIALS Over 20 years in high-tech manufacturing management, with increasing responsibility in production inventory control, purchasing, distribution, and business planning. Proven track record in development and implementation of computer-based manufacturing control systems.

Known as high-energy, results-oriented individual who works well under pressure, demonstrates good judgment. Respected for the ability to make sense out of complex situations and develop a sound action plan. Communicates clearly and makes outstanding personal presentations. Establishes effective client/customer relationships, inspires confidence and trust.

RELEVANT EXPERIENCE

[a]**Operations Management**
- Reduced manufacturing costs 30% by consolidating four plants into one.
- Achieved 105% shipment increase in 3 years, on-time deliveries at 90%.
- Established sales-operations forecast procedures, operations planning and integration to financial budget.
- Introduced four new products from prototypes on schedule, successfully co-ordinating marketing, engineering, and manufacturing startup.
- Computerized finished goods, factory service and branch operations, improving customer service, order processing, assembly, and distribution programs.

Materials
- Reduced inventory investment from $7 to $5 million in 1 year, while improving on-time deliveries from 80 to 96%.
- Established second sources for 'A' items, reducing purchase costs by 12%. Implemented scheduled delivery, stockless purchasing and vendor programs that covered 70% of annual volume.

(a) Experience is organized by type of activity

Karen Cox (continued)
404-687-9321

- In a 220-employee electromechanical plant, reduced inventory $1 million in 2 years, increasing turns from 3.3 to 5.5.

- Extensively revised materials sourcing strategies for four plants worldwide.

- Combined four distribution facilities at annual savings of $270,000.

Manufacturing
Control Systems

- Directed MRP implementation for multiplant operations, including master scheduling, inventory control, BMP, and shop floor control modules. Experience with IBM, PICS, MAN-MAN, and AMAPS packages.

- Performed operations audits, evaluation of procedures and systems. Defined appropriate system for future needs. Established steering committees, implementation teams, project planning, and performance criteria.

Organization
Development

- Assessed department capabilities and needs; established measurable goals and objectives; evaluated organization structure and implemented needed changes.

- Established first genuinely effective performance appraisals, upgraded and re-assigned staff, recruited new middle management. Resolved unsatisfactory performance from long-term employees.

- Provided senior industry management orientation to business school's external programs. Created and delivered custom programs for manufacturing and engineering managers in factory automation, technology update, MIS, finance, operations, and project management.

EMPLOYMENT

2002–Present
Director, Materials and Logistics, Pierce Manufacturing, Atlanta, GA 20502
A 900-employee high-tech manufacturer with 4 plants

1992–2002
Vice President Operations, Mohawk Corporation, Marietta, GA 30060
A 400-employee computer component manufacturer

1985–1992
Director of Corporate Manufacturing
Manager, Business and Operations Planning
Manager, Physical Distribution
Materials Manager

1983–1985
Staff Analyst, Computer Tech Company, Towson, MD 21204
A 30-person software consulting firm

1981–1983
Design Engineer, RCA, Pittsburgh, PA 15203

1979–1981
Field and Product Engineer, General Electric, Lynn, MA 01905

Karen Cox (continued)
404-687-9321

EDUCATION   University of Pittsburgh, School of Management, MBA—1983
                Graduated with honors. Nights

                University of Houston, BS—1979
                Electrical Engineering—dean's list
                Quality Assurance Certification in Testing

ASSOCIATIONS AND ACTIVITIES
                Member, American Production and Inventory Control Society
                (APICS)

                Member, Operations Management Association

                Guest speaker at APICS, Purchasing Management Association,
                University of Vermont and Merrimack College executive
                programs and seminars

PUBLICATIONS   "Breaking Ground in Materials Requirements Planning,"
                presented at 15th International APICS Convention, Las Vegas,
                Nevada 89501

PERSONAL   Hobbies include sailing, cross-country skiing, singing in
                church choir

EXHIBIT 6-4 • A Scannable Resume

A resume prepared for computerized scanning is a variation of a chronological resume that is
designed to contain lots of items that are easily picked out by an electronic screening program.

Betsy Percival
72 Rutgers Drive
Wilmington, DE
302-383-4702
Betsy_Percival@aol.com

SELECTED ACHIEVEMENTS

♦ **Earned 5 consecutive 100% club awards. Quota was increased by 20% each year.** (a)
♦ **22% revenue growth year-to-year, resulting in over $6,500,000 last year.**
♦ **Ranked in top 3% of entire field marketing force.**

SPECIAL SKILLS

New-product sales	Strategic sales
Relationship sales	New market development
Competitive sales contracts	High technology sales
Key account management	Contract negotiation
Executive sales presentation	Competitive product positioning
Product line management	Account planning
Fluent in Spanish	Cross-cultural skills

EXPERIENCE

1997 to Present   **National Lighting Corp.**, Wilmington, DE

Senior Marketing Representative
Key responsibilities include marketing all products and services to
customers in my assigned territory. Responsible for all customer satisfaction, account coverage needs, maintaining customer executive contacts, and quota attainment. Achieved 115% of assigned quota in 2000
and earned fifth consecutive 100% club award. In 2001 gained 100%
customer satisfaction on accounts surveyed and increased revenues by
$1,200,000, which represents a 22% increase over 1999. Total rev-
enues for 1990 totaled over $6,5000,000.

1991–97   *Marketing Representative*
Responsible for new accounts and first-time users of small to mid-
range computer systems. Sold and installed over 40 new accounts in
1996 which was the highest total for the Wilmington office in that
year. Earned the Golden Circle Award and 100% club. Only top 3% of
all reps qualify for the Golden Circle each year.

(a) Note the use of many figures and key words (such as *awards*, *increased*, *growth*, *ranked*) that are often
sought by screening programs. This type of resume is being used increasingly as the initial screening by
Internet, executive, and large company recruiters who deal with large numbers of applicants.

Betsy Percival
Page 2

1988–91   **Ingersoll Products**, Wilmington, DE
               Associate Marketing Representative
               Key objectives were to complete training and gain thorough
               understanding of the entire product line. Finished in the top 10%
               of class and was elected President of Sales School Class.

EDUCATION

               BBA, Clemson University, June 1988
               Major: Business Administration and Management, Marketing
               Minor: Computer Science
               Dean's List, Finished in Top 10% of Graduating Class

PROFESSIONAL ASSOCIATIONS

               President, Young Executives' Club, 1996
               Member, Chamber of Commerce
               Member, Marketing Management Association

COMMUNITY ACTIVITIES

               Board of Directors, Lenox Middle School
               Committee Member, United Way of Delaware

SALES EXPERIENCE

               Telemarketing, 1 yr.
               Forecasting, 5 yrs.
               Cold calling, 3 yrs.
               Market research, 2 yrs.
               One-on-One presentations, 5 yrs.
               Financial justifications, 5 yrs.
               Group presentations, 3 yrs.
               Executive marketing, 3 yrs.
               Technical sales, 5 yrs.

Your Accomplishments

Describe your experiences with PARs, which describe your accomplishments rather than responsibilities. The work you've done preparing your PARs pays off here. In a chronological resume, select your accomplishments of each job starting with your latest. Then prioritize them, listing the most important first. Prioritizing your PARs for each job is important—readers tend to skim your resume and may read only one or two accomplishments for each job you've held. In a functional resume, organize your PARs by function rather than by job.

Your Objective

An objective is optional if your summary clearly shows the type of job you're looking for. If you use an objective, make it broad, such as "operations management or financial executive," which inclines readers to think of their needs in your functional area. Don't use a job title such as Controller. It makes the reader focus on the title. If the company already has a good Controller, the reader is likely to dismiss the resume quickly.

Your Summary

A good summary (see Exhibit 6-1, Herbert Gleason), is usually the first thing that gets a reader's attention. Condense your experience into a few lines. Describe one or two highlights that are likely to get attention. Describe several of your skills and strengths. Here are two examples of summaries.In addition, the resumes shown in Exhibits 6-1 through 6-4 show several other examples of summaries.

Example 1

Seven years of experience as a CFO in software and financial services industries. Six years as an auditor with Coopers-Lybrand, advancing to senior level. In-depth experience in Latin America. Fluent in Spanish. Known as a hands-on manager and team builder with strong focus on the bottom line.

Example 2

Eight years of experience in the formation and execution of successful real estate developments, from initial conception through design, financing, and construction.

- Five years in managing construction on large projects and renovations
- Extensive experience in the following:

Budgeting and financial analysis	Lease and contract negotiations
Financing proposals and processes	Design and construction management
Asset management	State and local permitting

Your Education

Education is generally placed toward the end of a resume unless it's particularly strong. If it is, you can summarize it in the upper right corner of the first page (see Exhibit 6-1, Herbert Gleason's resume). This technique gives your education immediate attention without detracting from the summary and your most recent experience. You can add details at the end of the resume, such as your major (particularly if related to your work), honors, scholarships, and whether you earned your degree at night.

Dates

If you've already left your most recent job, you can show it as 2003–. If you graduated 25 years ago or more, consider omitting your graduation date. Also consider excluding experience more than 20 years old, summarizing it as "previous experience" without giving dates.

Length

Unless you have senior executive experience, limit your resume to two pages. Also write a one-page version, which can be useful in networking and blind prospecting. (See Exhibit 6-2, Fred Barkley's resume, for an example.)

TIPS ON WRITING RESUMES

Try to put your three or four most important items in the first half of the first page, in your most recent jobs or perhaps in the summary. This critical zone gets the reader's attention during his or her initial 15- to 30-second assessment.

Keep your resume readable, which means you should be selective in what you say about your experience. A crowded resume turns people off and can be ineffective. People shy away from reading a densely worded document. Another way of cutting down your resume is leaving off any experience that isn't really relevant to what you're seeking. Remember, the resume is a sales tool; it hits the highlights of your experience but doesn't include all of it.

PREPARING YOUR RESUME

Because preparing a top-notch resume takes time, prepare a temporary resume at the very start of your job search in case you're asked for one in the first few days. Explain that it's a draft. Taking the time to prepare an outstanding resume should be one of your first priorities. It may take several weeks to prepare and get it properly criticized. Minimizing the importance of a strong resume is risky, especially in midcareer.

For more examples of resumes, see *Best Resumes for $100,000+ Jobs* by Wendy S. Enelow, Impact Publications, 2001. Most resume books apply one basic format to perhaps a hundred different jobs, often without good summaries and using good PARs. Enelow's book, however, shows various effective resume formats, applicable to $100,000+ jobs, including a wide variety of good summary and PAR examples for numerous circumstances. Many are very suitable for jobs with high five-figure salaries. It also shows strong resumes for many different positions. Also collect copies of any resumes that you are particularly impressed by, noting especially how things are expressed.

In the first draft of your resume, include everything you think you may want in your final draft. Don't worry about the length or format at this time. Set the draft aside for a day or two, then review it, correcting it and adding to it as you see fit.

If your draft is three pages long, reduce it to two pages by eliminating the weakest items (usually your early experience) and by communicating the ideas in fewer words. Beware of squeezing your resume too much by reducing margins, type styles, and the like because you'll also reduce readability. In Enelow's book some resumes are too cramped with type that is too small and difficult to read. Often shorter resumes are more effective because the ideas are more readable, so the reader assimilates them more quickly.

Once you have the proper length, zero in on the format. Make sure the most important items stand out: the summary, your key qualifications, and your accomplishments. Use indentations, font size, bold or italic type, capital letters, short paragraphs, and numerals (rather than words) to get your message across more effectively. Remember that your resume has to be able to pass the 30-second test and also a careful, complete reading. Visually check your resume. Is it pleasant to the eye? Is there too much open space, or is it too cramped?

GETTING YOUR RESUME EFFECTIVELY CRITICIZED

Don't underestimate this step. Getting your resume criticized properly greatly improves your chances of getting your search off to a strong start. Refer to page 13, the story of Bill Martin's experience using a weak resume unsuccessfully for several months, then having a dramatic change in his fortunes with a new resume, emphasizes the importance of good criticism.

Getting your resume properly criticized starts with finding two or three people who are likely to do it effectively. Many people think they have special expertise in reviewing resumes, but unfortunately most people don't really know what to look for. Use your network of former job hunters or a good career workshop to find people who can really give useful criticism. Don't be surprised if you get different opinions on certain aspects of your resume. Consider all the suggestions; then use your judgment to do what you feel is best for you.

While getting good resume criticism is important, beware of stretching the time out too much in doing it. You'll get better criticism if you allow people time to review it at their leisure rather than asking them to critique it on the spot. Here are some questions for them to consider:

- Is my objective reasonable?
- Have I mentioned all the important functions for the kind of job I'm seeking?
- What can I leave out?
- Is the layout good? Easy to read? Are the explanations too wordy? Too densely worded?
- From reading this, what concerns would you have about me as a candidate?
- If you were reviewing resumes for the type of job I'm seeking, would you be likely to select mine for an interview? If not, why not?

You're undoubtedly anxious to start interviewing. However, don't start until you've gotten proper criticism and revised your resume accordingly. If you are working with a good outplacement firm, you would have your resume reviewed by three or four experts, and they would review several drafts. That's how important they feel the review process is!

SOME ADDITIONAL THOUGHTS ON RESUME TIPS

Describe your experience in simple, understandable language. Use short sentences. Use forceful, but simple, words. Avoid technical jargon unless you're a technically oriented person applying for a technical job.

Highlight key items with indentations, capital letters, underlining, boldface, or italic type.

Use different type styles to differentiate between your company, your division, and your position. If you don't show each classification differently, it makes it more difficult to quickly identify these items. For example:

• *Poor:*

> United States Machine Company
> > Hardware Division
> > Saginaw, MI
> > Market Research Analyst

• *Better:*

> UNITED STATES MACHINE COMPANY
> > Hardware Division
> > Saginaw, MI
> > <u>Market Research Analyst</u>

If your job title didn't describe your true responsibilities, clarify it. Executive Vice President was the title of the chief operating officer of XYZ—Italy. His boss was located in Paris and was the V.P. European Operations (and President of southern Europe). Why not use Chief Executive Officer (as Executive Vice President) of Italy?

For each company you've worked for, describe the company's size and the industry. Don't assume employers will recognize the company name, particularly in this era of mergers. Clarify it with something like "United Conglomerate (formerly XYZ Corp.)."

If your job titles don't describe your overall responsibilities, include a summary of your duties.

Talk about your latest position in the present tense: "Assistant General Manager" not "Was Assistant General Manager."

In your summary, include the name of any prestigious company you've worked for, such as General Electric.

If gender isn't clear,—for example, Li Micadale—precede your name with Ms. or Mr.

Define abbreviations and acronyms that potential employers might not know.

Define proper names. For example, "Harlan Prize" may have been a real scholastic honor, but it won't mean anything unless it's properly described: "Awarded to three seniors for outstanding scholarship and leadership."

Don't say, "Will furnish references on request."

Don't restrict the location—it could be a turnoff.

Include your fax number and e-mail address. Incidentally, check your voice mail message periodically to make sure it sounds the way you want it to.

Put your name and the page number on the top of the second and any subsequent pages.

Be sure to proofread your resume carefully, and ask someone else to proofread it also.

If you feel your resume is not getting reasonable results and don't understand why, you may be using it ineffectively or your expectations may be unrealistic.

MAJOR RESUME PROBLEMS

Here are the major problems related to resumes and what to do about them:

- *Your resume doesn't state accomplishments or doesn't state them effectively.* See page 61 on writing PARs.

- *The resume is too congested.* Try a more open format to make it as easy as possible for people to skim your resume and be impressed with your outstanding qualifications. Look at Exhibits 6-1 through 6-4 for easy-to-skim formats.

- *Your expectations for a rate response are unreasonable.* You're not setting reasonable results. Review your resume with a couple of your most valuable advisors. Discuss with them how you're using it.

- *Your resume is too technical.* Review your resume to reduce technical jargon. Even if you are looking for a technical or semitechnical job, many nontechnical and semitechnical people will still be reading your resume. Don't confuse or turn them off.

- *Your resume reflects the jobs you've had in the past, not the job you want now.* Lieutenant Colonel Francis Townsend retired from the Army after 20 years and got an MBA. He had to convince a civilian employer that his administrative, diplomatic, and command experience in the military was comparable to what might be required of him in industry. His original resume was worded in military terms, and his MBA was buried at the end, giving the impression of an experienced military officer with no particular business credentials. When he switched to a functional resume emphasizing his recent MBA and described his 12 years of Army experience in business terms, he quickly got an interview and a position as Assistant Operations Manager of a $500 million company.

- *Your resume buries your most relevant experience.* Ed Fisher wanted to make a career change. In the last four years, he had import and export positions with two companies. In the four years before that, he was Chief Operating Officer of a foreign subsidiary with 8000 employees and had set sales and profit records. Although his earlier experience was stronger, it was on the second page of his resume. Most prospective employers probably missed it, putting his resume in the "not-interested" pile before they finished the first page. He revised the resume and put this outstanding experience in the summary. He also emphasized it in a cover letter resulting in two good offers fairly quickly.

Once you've gotten your resume polished, use it aggressively. Correct any serious errors immediately. Otherwise note any criticisms you get on it. If it isn't achieving the results you want after a month, incorporate the relevant criticism and get another critique by the one or two people whose earlier suggestions were most useful.

CHAPTER 7

NETWORKING

HOW ARE YOU LIKELY TO GET YOUR JOB?

This chapter and the following two discuss the ways to get your job. It divides the ways into the *hidden* and *visible job markets* and tells you how to use them effectively. This chapter is on networking, and the following chapter is on blind prospecting. These are the two hidden job markets. Both allow you to *take charge of your job search* by retaining the initiative. When you approach enough companies of your choosing, ultimately you will reach several who will see in your experience someone who can fill an often unrecognized need the company has. Combined these two approaches are the most successful for most midcareer job hunters, as you'll see below.

Chapter 9, "The Visible Market," explains how to be most successful in the visible market, which covers responding to jobs that are being actively recruited for. This is principally the recruiting done by executive search firms and similar recruiters, answering ads and Internet recruiting. The thorough screening methods of the visible market are designed to identify "the best" candidates from a large pool. Unless you're among the elite—that is, the roughly 10 percent sought by such recruiters—you're unlikely to get much interest from any of these activities. Therefore, most of your time is much better spent pursuing the hidden market.

DBM (formerly Drake, Beam, Morin), one of the largest outplacement firms, made a survey of over 28,000 successful job hunters in 2001 to identify how they got their jobs. The results are as follows:

Blind prospecting	3%
Internet	5%
Advertisements	6%
Search firm or agency	9%
Networking	61%
Other or unknown	16%

This survey was also broken down by gender and age (over and under 50) with each category having quite similar results. Eliminating the 16 percent of the "unidentified" results, 73 percent got their jobs by networking. Undoubtedly the Internet is the fastest-growing source although its success rate is still small compared with the probable effort people spend accessing it. The DBM results are in line with a number of other such surveys.

You should use the survey's results as a guideline for allocating your time to each of these activities. So roughly three-fourths of your time should be spent networking. Few other job-hunting books explain networking as a separate subject. It is done in this book because it is the method most likely to lead to success for you.

The object is to get meetings with important people you know and pyramid them by getting introductions to others (known as referrals) for help on your search and possible leads. Almost all job hunters do some networking, many do a lot of it. Some do it very effectively, but many can improve how they do it. You'll be shown how to carry it out using a 12-step process. You're probably taking many of these steps already, but you'll be shown how to carry them out better and you'll also be shown some useful steps that you're probably not taking now.

This 12-step networking program consists of the following 12 steps:

* Enlarging your list of contacts
* Getting networking interviews with them
* Preparing for networking interviews
* Building rapport in networking interviews
* Being alert to hidden job possibilities
* Getting good referrals
* Getting good information on referrals
* Getting personally introduced to referrals
* Giving something back in return
* Getting more candid criticism
* Developing a continuing relationship
* Analyzing interview results and followup

Some contacts you meet with may be so impressed with your experience that they may identify an unrecognized need they have for which you may be the first and so far only candidate. In this case, the company may even tailor a job to meet some of your needs. Mark Granovetter, professor of sociology at Stanford University, identified an important facet of hidden jobs when his survey concluded that 43.4 percent of them were created at the approach of the job hunter (in Mark Granovetter, *Getting a Job: A Study of Contacts and Careers*, 2nd ed., Chicago, IL, University of Chicago Press, 1995). Have realistic expectations though; you may have to contact a lot of people before such a hidden job comes to light. Unless the interviewer indicates a serious hiring need, don't push it—being too aggressive could be a real turnoff, not to mention a breech of your implicit promise in asking for his or her help when you approached him or her. Other byproducts of a networking meeting may be that the contact knows of an open job and even recommends you to a friend who is trying to fill a position.

You increase your chances of networking successfully by developing considerable skill at it. Key people are less likely to spend time with job hunters than they were a decade ago because they're approached more frequently and have more demanding jobs. Networking is still very much alive though—it often just takes more skill than it used to. Effective networkers still get excellent results. Many key people defy the old adage "A friend in need is a friend indeed." Many feel more like the statement of a CEO of a Fortune 100 company: "A friend in need is a pain in the butt."

To get the best help in networking, a job hunter must earn that help by being thoroughly professional in all dealings with a contact, whether the contact is close or distant. Job hunters must also be well prepared to describe their experience effectively and conduct themselves knowledgeably and intelligently. They must also be skillful in responding to weaknesses in their backgrounds.

Any given contact may be either quite helpful or not helpful at all. How contacts respond to you depends on your relationship to them, your experience, the impression you make on them, and how busy they are at that moment.

Always bear in mind that your contact, when he or she makes a referral, has a relationship with the referral and wants to protect that relationship. If your contact thinks you might hurt that relationship in any way, you won't get the referral. Remember, you are your contact's representative to the referral.

ENLARGING YOUR LIST OF CONTACTS

Some job hunters say, "I don't have many contacts." Some job hunters whose best chance of getting a good job is by networking have the smallest, least useful networks to tap into. These people must work hard to expand their networks. They need to make an exhaustive list of their contacts; they will probably find that they have more than they think.

Some job hunters say, "I don't want to use my friends." Suppose that the position of you and a friend were reversed: Someone you know is job hunting and needs help that you're well positioned to give. Do you think your friend would contact you under the circumstances? Of course, he or she would. Your friends, relatives, and acquaintances are certainly the most useful sources of help in your job search; you can't afford not to use them. You may find you even enhance your relationship with them.

The first step in networking is to develop your list of contacts. This list is preliminary; you may never contact some of the people on it. At this stage though, include as many names as possible. Typically job hunters are uncomfortable including certain names for various reasons, but as they network, they become more comfortable approaching people they were reluctant to contact at first. So list every person you know who might possibly be helpful. Decide later what order you want to contact them in. Put the following types of people on your list.

Business friends	College friends
Accountants	Salespeople
Consultants	Competitors
Customers	Insurance agents
Bankers	Fund-raisers
Politicians	Professors
Doctors	Members of civic groups
Attendees at community meetings	Neighbors
Volunteers	Exercise partners
Relatives	E-mail acquaintances
Casual acquaintances	Company executives
Former associates (superiors, peers, subordinates)	High school friends
	Suppliers
	Lawyers

Stockbrokers	Social friends
Ministers	Fellow commuters
Parishioners	Members of same ethnic
Other parents at your	group
children's activities	

You'd be surprised at some of the people known by those who provide personal services to you: your barber, hairdresser, massage therapist, personal trainer, and so on. Some job hunters have gotten the key lead from one of them.

You can get particularly good help from some recent and present job hunters. They're empathetic and particularly knowledgeable of sources, people, and techniques they've found effective. Once you start building your list, you'll recall other contacts at odd times, such as driving in the car, watching TV, or in the middle of the night. Keep a notebook handy to jot the names down while you think of them.

The concept of market niches is helpful in building your list. For example, electrical engineers have special knowledge about the market for electrical engineers, and alumni of certain colleges help fellow alumni. Job hunters get particular support from others with like backgrounds.

If you hesitate to contact casual acquaintances, ask yourself these questions:

• Could this person help me?

• Is this person likely to call me? If not, then why shouldn't I initiate the call?

• What's the risk?

  • Am I afraid of getting turned down?

  • Do I really think the contact may be affronted?

  • Will I be disappointed if nothing happens?

• What's stopping me from making this call?

Others who don't know a particular contact as well as you may be getting just the kind of help you need.

Put on your list anyone you know who is likely to know other people who could help you. To develop your list, search your business and personal address and phone books, social acquaintances, alumni directory, trade association memberships, club memberships, previous calendars, and so on. You need to build a long list to develop a full calendar, say 7 to 10 appointments a week. Classify your contacts as follows:

A. The 5 to 10 people whom you're closest to and who are the best situated

B. The next 25 people meeting the priorities in A

C. The rest

Many people make the mistake of trying to see all of the A contacts first. If you haven't networked in recent years, you need some practice to get up to speed. Therefore, start by seeing, say, eight people, perhaps six C's and two B's. Get more comfortable with the process and with common questions and roadblocks so that you'll be more effective with your A's and B's. Next approach a couple of A's who know you best, people who are likely to be more forgiving and particularly candid. Tell them you're starting to network, and ask them to be forthright in telling you how you come across and in pointing out particular shortcomings you may have and ways to counteract them. Next ask them if you can see them in a couple of weeks to review your progress. Then try some people in areas you want to target. Incidentally, many job hunters find that many of their A's were not as helpful as they expected and that several of the B's and C's were much more so.

Carry personal business cards with you for exchanging with people at various meetings.

Practice your *elevator drill*—getting help through chance acquaintances. Imagine you're riding an elevator in a large office building. Suddenly a key person you know gets on, somebody you know but haven't seen in several years. Be prepared to tell this person about your situation in a few minutes, say, the time it takes to ride up in the elevator. After brief pleasantries you should say the following:

(This is what I have been doing in my last job.)

"Bert, you probably don't know it, but I'm currently in a career transition. Perhaps you remember I was Assistant Vice President of Sales at Munson Networks. Recently I've been let go in a typical shuffle."

(This is what I am looking for.)

"I'm in the process of looking for a job as a sales manager of a high-tech company."

(Here is a brief description of my experience.)

"My early career was in direct selling of peripherals. For the past four years I have been primarily involved in selecting and training our 150-person sales force at Munson and dealing with our largest accounts."

(Here's what's unique about me.)

"My particular strengths are in recruiting and motivating a sales force and in direct selling."

(Here is how you can help me.)

"I would like to meet with you for a few minutes. I don't expect you'll have a job or know of one. I'm looking for advice and information. Would you be willing to see me?"

Frequently, this chance encounter results in the person's agreeing to a meeting.

Some job hunters draw into a shell and avoid gatherings where they might meet people who can be helpful. Withdrawing is a natural reaction, but it only hurts you. Take every opportunity to see people, and don't be bashful about asking for help though doing it discreetly: at church, community and business meetings, social events, watching Little League games, and so on. Sometime in the future, some of these people may ask to see you when the shoe is on the other foot.

GETTING INTERVIEWS WITH CONTACTS

Decide whether to approach contacts by letter or by phone. Call anyone you know well on the telephone. Write a letter to someone you know only slightly or don't know at all and follow it up with a phone call. (See Exhibit 7-1 for a sample letter.) Make sure you make the follow-up call promptly—or the recipient may have put you out of his or her mind.

When you call, you may reach the referral's voice mail, or you may reach a gatekeeper or the referral directly.

Reaching Voice Mail

Reaching someone's voice mail is frequent these days, so develop skill in dealing with it. Use the technique of *accelerating pressure*. On your first call, leave your name, the name of your referral (Don Weinberg), the reason for your call, your phone number, the message you'll call back in two or three days, and a thank-you for this help in advance. *Keep control of the telephoning so you don't get called back when you're not near your phone or when it's inconvenient.*

Follow up with another call in two to three days. Leave the same information as before but add your relationship to your contact and that person's reason for referring you. If you don't get through to the referral on the third call, call his or her assistant. Ask the assistant to put you through. Learning how to deal with these gatekeepers is extremely important.

EXHIBIT 7-1 • A Letter Approaching a Referral

June 1, 2003

Mr. Frederick Mancuso
Senior Vice President
Albert Software Company
435 Fulton Street
Milwaukee, WI 53062

Dear Mr. Mancuso:

Don Weinberg of Marietta, a fellow director of the American Marketing Association here, suggested that I contact you for advice. Recently I left Burlo Networks as their National Marketing Manager, and I am seeking a new opportunity.

Based on my diverse background and experience with high-end to low-end software and network products designed for many industries, I feel confident that I can make a valuable contribution toward new-product planning, market development, and market expansion for a high-tech firm.

My extensive experience over the last 17 years has required the ability not only to develop and market packaged and customized software in domestic and international markets but also to provide the support products for end users at all levels. Because of this diversity, I feel able to transfer my skills to marketing many other products.

I do not expect you to know of any openings, but I would like your advice. In the next few days I will call you to see whether we can have a 15-minute meeting. Enclosed is a copy of my resume, which provides you with more details of my background.

Sincerely,

Mary A. Jensen
178 Monroe Street
Madison, WI 53704

608-535-7943

Reaching a Gatekeeper

One of a gatekeeper's key roles is to decide which calls to put through. This assistant uses knowledge of the boss's wishes, his or her friends, and workload in handling somebody unknown. The gatekeeper wants to know whether the caller has an appropriate connection to the boss and a legitimate need to speak with him or her.

Further information you may be asked to give are the following:

+ Whether the boss expects your call
+ Whether the boss knows you personally
+ Whether the boss will know what the call is about

Doing research on the referral is important to get past the gatekeeper and gain access to the referral, as well as for the interview itself. Getting information about these people can be difficult. Your best source is to ask your original contact about the referral:

+ How do you spell the person's name (if unusual)?
+ What's the name of his or her company and his or her position?
+ What's your relationship with him or her?
+ Why do you feel this person could help me? (You're looking for an answer such as, "He's an expert on the networking industry's problems in the Pacific Rim.")
+ Ask for some personal information, for example, "Is Fred a golfer like you, Don?" Sometimes you'll get lucky and get a revealing answer: "Oh no, he's probably at his camp in New Hampshire and climbing mountains."

Other resources for information about Fred are friends, suppliers, lawyers, bankers, and so on, but you probably can get all the information you need from Don, and more easily.

The gatekeepers may try to put you off by saying, "Mr. Mancuso doesn't take employment calls." You can say, "That makes sense, but this isn't an employment call. I am not trying to get a job at your company. Don Weinberg of Marietta felt that Mr. Mancuso could be helpful in giving me his ideas on the software industry's main problems in the Pacific Rim. I'd like to meet with him for 15 minutes, any time in the next two weeks. Would you check with him to see if Thursday, April 27, at 9:45 would be convenient? I'll call back tomorrow for his answer."

It's usually easier to get in to see key people by saying you need only 15 minutes and asking for it well in the future, when the person feels less pressure about his or her schedule. Suggesting a time such as 9:45 implies that Fred can schedule a 10:00 appointment. Be prepared for this "15 minutes" to last an hour or more; it probably won't, but it could. However, you can accomplish a lot in 15 minutes if you use the time efficiently.

Reaching the Contact Directly

If you have good luck and reach the referral directly, be prepared for one of several responses:

"I just can't see you now. I'm too busy. I'm about to go off on vacation [or on a business trip or to a sales meeting, etc.]."

"We're not hiring at this time."

"I don't know of any jobs that would be suitable."

"I can't think of any contacts I could suggest for you."

Use the same basic strategy you used with the gatekeeper. Reply to a specific obstacle. For example, "I understand that you do not have any openings, but Don Weinberg, a close friend and neighbor for 10 years, thought your advice could be helpful, particularly about software problems in the Pacific Rim. I'm looking only for 15 minutes of your time. Could we do it at 9:45, April 28?"

Here are some additional ways to improve your success in gaining access to key people.

Try hard to get a personal interview. If you're turned down, ask for a few minutes on the phone. "This matter can be handled easily on the phone. Do you have time now, or should we set a time for me to call back?" Conducting telephone interviews is discussed on page 108.

- Try to avoid the gatekeeper by calling early in the morning or late in the afternoon or at lunch time.

- Write down any rebuffs you haven't heard before and prepare answers for them.

- List common problems gaining access, and discuss them with one or two salespeople, who are experts at dealing with such problems.

- Tape a few of your phone calls, with the other person's permission. Get the conversation criticized by your spouse or a friend.

- If you're unsuccessful gaining access to an important referral, consider calling your contact back to ask him or her to intercede for you.

- If you're having good success in getting meetings with referrals, try approaching the assistant first.

PREPARING FOR NETWORKING INTERVIEWS

To build a favorable relationship with a contact, you must have some knowledge of his or her company and its problems. Knowing the company's problems and recent changes in operations is particularly useful in conversing intelligently and asking pertinent questions. This improves your chances of developing good rapport with the contact. How to research this information is explained on page 142, "Researching the Company."

For your interview with Fred, prepare a list of four or five questions about the company's problems and operations related to your field of expertise, such as the following:

* About the company

  "What has Albert Co. done about your loss of business in the Pacific Rim?"

  "Which countries do you think will recover most quickly?"

* About your search

  "Do you see anything in my background that would concern potential employers?"

  "What skills and personal qualities do you feel are the most important in my field?"

  "What sort of company [or industry] would be most interested in my experience?"

Bring a notebook with you and take notes. By doing this, you're signaling, "This is important to me."

BUILDING RAPPORT IN NETWORKING INTERVIEWS

When you first meet Fred, try to chat about a couple of personal interests of his. Listen carefully and observe the things in the person's office, such as pictures and objects on the desk. After a couple of minutes of small talk, you should start off by saying something like:

"Fred, I really appreciate your willingness to see me and help me with my career transition. Right off I want you to understand that I realize it's highly unlikely that you have an opening I'd be considered for or know of one."

How effectively you conduct yourself in the first few minutes of the interview often determines whether you get the contact's best response or just a routine one. Fred may start by saying, "Tell me about yourself." This is an opportunity to use your two-minute introduction (page 142). If you aren't asked for it and Fred doesn't know you well professionally, volunteer it. Don't assume the interviewer has spent any time with your resume. The beginning of the interview is usually focused on your agenda, so use the time profitably. End your introduction by saying, "That gives you a quick overview of who I am and what I'm looking for. " Then pause.

The interviewer usually responds by saying, "Of course, we don't have anything here for you." Then he is likely either to ask for more information on some aspect of your experience or start talking about his company. There will follow some give-and-take on his choice. Ask the most pertinent questions you've prepared. Have several copies of your resume in case you're asked for them.

BEING ALERT TO HIDDEN JOB POSSIBILITIES

Listen carefully to show that you're interested. Make intelligent comments and ask pertinent questions. Given the opportunity, use expanded PARs to demonstrate your experience, particularly in any area of the interviewer's interest. Most of the PARs in your resume are two-line bulleted statements. During your interview, expand them to two or three minutes, describing the problem you faced and the action you took including the skills you used. If the company has problems in your area of expertise, there may be a possibility of a hidden job. Explore the company's needs delicately because you promised in your initial approach that you wouldn't expect a job opportunity. You lose credibility if you push too hard.

The interview may turn into a preliminary job interview, even though you were told none existed. It may also turn into a discussion of your doing consulting for the company. Signs of this transition are the interviewer's asking increasingly probing questions about your background. This may indicate that a "green light" has turned on, with his or her revealing "insider information" about the company, introducing you to others in the company, extending the meeting beyond the time you expected, inviting you to come back, describing the company in a favorable way, or probing deeply about your salary expectations.

Handle questions about salary carefully. Revealing a specific figure too early could cool the company's interest in you or lock you into a salary below what is possible. At this point, say, "Salary is important, but it's only one consideration. The most important consideration is the opportunity itself."

Let the contact do most of the talking with your role being that of an interested and involved listener.

The better the rapport you develop, the greater the chance of a hidden job opening up and, if not, of your getting more and better referrals, better advice, and an opportunity to develop a continuing relationship.

GETTING GOOD REFERRALS

After exploring the unlikely chance of a hidden job and getting some general advice, your goal in networking is to get as many good referrals as you can. Try to get at least two referrals from every networking interview. Don't ask for referrals at the beginning of an interview. Make a good impression so that the contact offers referrals without your requesting them. Some key people are reluctant to give referrals these days because it's an imposition and puts the contact in the position of possibly wanting a reciprocal referral.

The best results in networking are realized by a subtle approach. Emphasize that you're seeking advice and information, easy things for the contact to give. As the conversation evolves and the contact gets to know you professionally, the contact will become more comfortable in giving you referrals and possible job leads.

There are several ways to prompt referrals without directly asking for them.

For example, take a list of 8 to 10 companies that you'd like to be introduced to. Ask your contact to review the list and comment on them. This approach often prompts the contact to offer names of people in a couple of the companies—names he or she probably wouldn't have volunteered otherwise.

Also, have a list of several questions to stimulate his or her thinking:

"Can you think of any companies that might need help in marketing in the telecommunications field?"

"Perhaps you know of a turnaround situation in which there's a real need for biotech research expertise."

"Can you think of any companies with a new head of operations in the last couple of months who might be reorganizing his or her staff?"

Finally, if you haven't had any success in getting referrals to this point, you might say, "I have been strongly encouraged by several people to get at least two referrals from every person I talk to. Whom would you suggest?"

Fred Mancuso might say, "A good person for you to see is Sara Barca, Vice President of Ace Software."

GETTING GOOD INFORMATION ON REFERRALS

Before you approach any referral, make sure you have your contact's permission to use his or her name, and ask your contact some pertinent questions about the referral to improve your chances of gaining access. Your best opportunity to get information on a referral is from Fred (the referrer). The type of questions that are most useful in gaining the cooperation of the gatekeeper are those already cited on page 97.

GETTING PERSONALLY INTRODUCED TO REFERRALS

If you've been having difficulty gaining access to your referrals, ask your contact to introduce you. You might ask, "Do you have any idea how hard it is to get an appointment with someone like Sara?" Fred

might react by saying, "I'm sure it may be very difficult. I'll call her."
Fred's call increases your chances of getting a meeting with her. If
Fred is willing to make an introductory call for you, find out whether
you're to call him back or wait for him to call you.

The purposes of trying to get your contact to make the referral are
the following:

◆ It makes it more likely that you'll get a meeting.

◆ In asking Sara to meet with you, Fred has to justify a reason for
   the favor, a form of preselling. He might say something like, "I'd
   appreciate the favor. Mary is quite an impressive person." This
   may not help much, but it doesn't hurt.

Sometimes your contact may make one or two calls for you while
you're in his office. Another thing he or she may do is write several
letters of introduction to the referrals.

Make the most of every opportunity to meet with a key person.
You never know which ones are going to pay off. Jack Freeman was
offered a meeting with Frank Logan of Mercury Systems, which was
several hours' drive away. Jack made the trip nevertheless. It seemed
to have been a waste of time. Six weeks later, Jack got called for an
interview with Ted Harris of Acme Software in another state, and this
interview led to an excellent offer. Ted told Jack that he had learned
of him through a good recommendation from Frank. Sometimes job
hunters get a good lead from someone they thought they had struck
out with.

GIVING SOMETHING BACK IN RETURN

Networking is usually used mistakenly by the job hunter as a one-
way street; the job hunter seeks help, and the contact gives it. Instead,
express your appreciation tangibly. Reciprocating is courteous and
professional. Furthermore, to the extent that you can help a contact,
you improve the likelihood that you'll get better help in return and

possibly develop a hidden job or a long-term relationship. In the course of the conversation, you may find that your contact needs something you can supply. Here are some of the things you can offer a contact:

• An introduction for the contact, an associate, or family member

• A news item or article

• The names of useful companies: vendors, competitors, new players in the field

• Information on a problem the contact has raised

In her first interview with the CEO of a venture started by a large firm of professionals, Jackie Martin was asked for her ideas on several aspects of the venture. After the interview she developed a 20-page business plan for the venture, including approaches to the specific aspects she was asked about, and sent it to the CEO, Tom DeLorenzo. He was very favorably impressed by her plan and her initiative. After several more interviews, she was hired as Tom's COO. Tom later told Jackie that her initiative in preparing the business plan got her a strong leg up on the other candidates.

GETTING MORE CANDID CRITICISM

All of the people you meet in interviews evaluate you, at least unconsciously, as to whether you have a credible objective, how good a candidate you are, and how effectively you present yourself. Their evaluation and related advice could be very helpful, but they rarely give it, particularly if it could be perceived as being critical. If you can set them at ease, they might be willing to give you more candid advice.

Jim Gordon, at about 30, was a pretty successful sales manager when he had a job interview with Bill Robinson, the CEO of a medium-sized company. During the interview, Bill turned to him and said, "Jim, you make a really blah impression." The remark shocked

Jim. Later Jim realized what a favor Bill had done for him in making him realize he wasn't as effective getting himself across as he thought. Wouldn't it be wonderful if you could get some of the impressive people you network with to be as candid with you in this way?

To get this type of criticism, try this tactic toward the end of the interview:

REED: May I ask you for an additional piece of advice?

MAC: Sure.

REED: I've heard of someone who got a candid and extremely helpful comment in an interview." [He then related the "blah impression" story.] You've been helpful, and I appreciate it. You've heard me describe what I am trying to do and my background. You've seen me in action. Are there one or two things that you've observed about me that would concern you if I were here as a job candidate? Please be candid. I would view it as a real favor.

Another option is to ask, "If you were considering hiring someone for the kind of job I'm looking for, what would you see as my strengths and my weaknesses?" or, "How would you rank me? Why wouldn't you rank me higher?"

If you make a poor impression on one person, you've probably been making one on others as well. Being aware of this problem will enable you to work on correcting it.

The "invitation to criticism" technique may make the contact more candid. This process can be powerful, but you should be selective in whom you use it with. You'll probably feel more comfortable using it with people with whom you've developed a good rapport.

DEVELOPING A CONTINUING RELATIONSHIP

As you network, do blind prospecting, and go to job interviews, you realize that you've seen some people who stand out as having been particularly helpful. Try to develop a continuing relationship with these contacts. As an interview is drawing to a close, every contact wants to ease you out and get on with his or her next commitment. Thank him, say how valuable the meeting has been, and ask if you can call in about a month. Most people will say yes even though you may not get through when you actually call. Within a day of the interview, hand-write a brief thank-you note to be courteous and build a continuing relationship. An example is shown in Exhibit 7-2.

After you've seen each referral, say, Sam Taylor, drop the original contact, Gerry Fulton, a note (handwritten or e-mailed) to relate the result of the meeting with the referral, and again express appreciation. This practice is a low-key way of keeping your name before the contact, shows your professionalism, and may make it easier to get additional help from this contact again. The more favorable the impression you make, the more likely you'll get more help. The contact will let you know if you're overdoing it.

EXHIBIT 7-2 • A Networking Thank-You Letter

June 1, 2004

Mr. Gerald F. Fulton
Executive Vice President
Ajax Industries
436 North Road
San Antonio, TX 78212

Dear Mr. Fulton:

I really appreciate your meeting with me today. Your insight on the networking problems in the Pacific Rim and your advice to broaden my networking were particularly helpful.

Your referrals to Sam Tyler of Omega Transport and Mary Turner of Maroon Guidance should be useful. I look forward to meeting both of them. They sound really knowledgeable in marketing linkage services. I left messages on their voice mail today. After I've seen them, I'll let you know the results.

Sincerely,

Nathan Chu

ANALYZING INTERVIEW RESULTS AND FOLLOWUP

Immediately after each such interview, you should record notes on the key things that you may want to remember for the future:

* Your referral's interests
* What seemed to be his priorities
* Things you might help him with
* Names and information he gave you on referrals
* The date (if any) for followup

The final thing you should do is take five minutes to ask yourself, "If I were going into the interview now, knowing what I do, what would I have done differently?" Learning as much as you can from each interview in your search will add considerably to your job hunting skills. If you've learned something to do or to avoid, add it to your preparation checklist for future networking interviews.

CONDUCTING TELEPHONE INTERVIEWS WHEN REFERRALS WON'T SEE YOU

If a referral won't grant you a personal interview, you should try to convert your call into a telephone interview. This type of interview usually isn't as useful as one that is face to face, but it can help, and it's all you'll probably get anyway. Telephone interviews are less effective because it's harder to

* Develop rapport over the phone
* Judge things that are happening on your contact's end
* Size up the contact
* Develop a relationship that might lead to a hidden job
* Develop a continuing relationship
* Get good referrals
* Get candid criticism

But none of these things should stand in your way of making the most of the opportunity. Sometimes a phone interview can be very useful—and you've got nothing to lose. Start a phone interview with an abbreviated introduction, of, say, one minute. Clarify your objective; state how the contact can help you. The dialog will be similar to the dialog in a face-to-face interview, but will probably be fairly brief.

Your approach to Jane Farrell in a phone interview might go like this:

"I appreciate your willingness to talk with me. Let me tell you what I'm trying to do and a little bit about my background. I have a BS in computer science from Indiana State and an MBA from the University of Illinois. Most recently I've been the European Sales VP at Interlogistics, where I was primarily involved in developing a network of distributors in western and southern Europe. We lived in Geneva for three years. I'm fluent in French and passable in German. Over five years I developed this segment from 3 percent of the company's sales to over 5 percent, even though the company's overall business was growing rapidly. Before Interlogistics, I was at Concept Software for seven years as International Sales Manager." I'd appreciate any advice you could give me in trying to relocate back to the States."

Let Jane select the direction she'd like the interview to take—perhaps discussing her business or asking a question about your experience. Your objectives are to try to convert your phone chat to a personal meeting (which is unlikely) and get referrals. Be prepared with some questions such as the following:

"What are the biggest problems your company is having increasing your business in Europe?"

"Can you think of any companies that might be in need of help in developing business abroad, particularly in the Europe?"

After a few minutes, you should focus on getting specific advice on your job search:

> "What do you see as problems in my getting assimilated in a U.S. company after five years overseas? My wife and I are concerned about our teenage children's education and want to move back to the States. I feel my experience can benefit a company in dealing with some of the changes going on in Europe. I'm willing to do a reasonable amount of traveling."

> "Do you have any thoughts on how to get a job here with my background?"

If you haven't received any referrals by this point, you should ask for them.

Be prepared with some general questions to keep the conversation going. Then as the interview seems to be winding down, thank the interviewer. Then ask, "In a month, if I'm still looking, may I call you to see if you have any further thoughts?"

CHAPTER 8

BLIND PROSPECTING

OVERVIEW

Blind prospecting is closely related to networking. The basic difference is that you have no previous connection with the people you're approaching. You should approach the CEO in small companies and the Vice President of your function in medium and large ones. Your contacting them is advertising your experience in the hope that they will recognize you as a possible candidate to fill a need they have. Because you have no direct or indirect relationship with these prospects, your rate of getting interviews is generally considerably lower than it would be in networking. If done well, however, blind prospecting can be quite rewarding. In fact, a blind prospect who will see you tends to be a more productive contact than your average networking contact because he agrees to see you for a possible need he may have for your experience in the company. A networking referral most often will see you as a courtesy to the person who made the referral and is less likely to be interested in you as a candidate for a job.

In blind prospecting, if the target executive happens to interview you when he or she has a need, you may be the first—and sometimes the only candidate—for a hidden job. For highly marketable people, blind prospecting can be a fast way to get a new job, and for anybody else it can be a good connection to productive leads if you do enough of it and do it effectively.

EXHIBIT 8-1 • Specific Preparation Steps in Blind Prospecting

	Target Letter Mailings	Telephone Prospecting	Broadcast Letters
List of companies	25–50 per mailing	100–200	1000
Identify specific individual	Yes	Yes	Yes
Information needed	Name of company Name of executive and title Address Telephone number	Name of company Name of executive and title Telephone number	Name of company Name of executive and title Address
Research needed	Research What company does, its size, scope, problems	Research (minimum) What company does and size	None
Means of contact	Specific letter to each company	Same telephone script	Same letter for all companies

The objective of blind prospecting is similar to that of networking: The first is to try to get a face-to-face meeting, and if that fails, the second is to get a phone interview.

As shown in Exhibit 8-1, there are three methods of blind prospecting:

1. *Target letters* are mailed to 25 to 50 companies simultaneously. Each letter consists of two sections: a carefully crafted introduction related to the company's specific problems and a description of your credentials. A strong target letter can produce quite good results. Followup phone calls are placed to the targeted companies soon after the letters are sent.

2. *Telephone prospecting* involves making calls to 100 to 200 companies. A calling campaign by a skilled "telemarketer" often is productive. Salespeople with good track records often find this to be a particularly useful approach.

3. A *broadcast letter* is the mailing of a "hard-sell" letter to perhaps 1000 companies on the chance that some of them may have a need for someone with your qualifications.

Here are four steps common to all blind prospecting methods:

1. Develop a list of companies to contact.
2. Identify the specific individuals to contact and how to contact them.
3. Conduct the appropriate research on the companies.
4. Prepare the letters for target and broadcast mailings and the script for phone prospecting.

Of the three alternatives, target letters are the most practical unless you can download someone else's file containing lists of contacts onto your computer in a usable format.

TARGET LETTER MAILINGS

Using this method of blind prospecting, you send individually con-structed letters to selected companies and follow up with a telephone call requesting an interview. Target 25 to 50 companies in a batch. You're better off to approach a manageable number rather than spreading yourself too thin. As shown in Exhibit 8-2, the letter you send relates your experience that is relevant to each company's prob-lems, as identified by your research. Follow up by phone three or four days later. A favorable response to such a letter indicates some level of interest and may result in an interview. Make sure you do a thorough job of researching the company.

TELEPHONE PROSPECTING

With the same amount of effort, you can approach many more exec-utives by phone than by a mailing followed up by phone. Telemar-keting is hard and often discouraging work, but if you're sharp on the

EXHIBIT 8-2 • Target Letter

February 1, 2003

Mr. Jerome Goldstein
President and Chief Executive Officer
Advanced Magnetics, Inc.
61 Mooney Street
Canton, OH 44702

Dear Mr. Goldstein:

I have read with great interest the significant results being achieved by Advanced Magnetics in recent months, including the receipt of progress payments from Squibb, the NDS filings for Gastromark and Feridex, and the European launch of Lumirem. The company has clearly established strong momentum. As a senior financial manager, I would like to help you and the entire Advanced Magnetics team in sustaining that momentum in the years ahead.

I am particularly interested in the position of CFO or Deputy CFO. My background is detailed in the attached résumé, with the following highlights:

♦ 16 years of financial experience, including treasury, controllership, and investor relations

♦ Most recently Vice President and Corporate Controller for Mercury Instruments

♦ Experience in small entrepreneurial environments

♦ BS, engineering, Princeton University; MBA, University of Virginia

♦ Outstanding references from all previous employers

I would greatly appreciate a brief introductory meeting. I will call in a few days to arrange one.

Sincerely,

---

phone, skillful in overcoming roadblocks, and have a highly marketable background, it can be a fast way of getting a job. Many salespeople use it successfully. It may be worth a try.

Success depends on the marketability of your background, the number of calls you make, how effectively you reach target executives, and how effectively you present yourself.

♦ Block out several hours for each phoning session. You tend to develop a rhythm in such an activity. Test results at several times of the day to see what time to call is most productive.

- Briefly record the result of each call.

- Review the results after every 10 calls, modifying your approach accordingly. What can you do to make your phone prospecting more effective?

- Prepare a good answer to any new roadblock you encounter so that you can deal with it effectively next time.

- Tape your end of the phone conversations to see how effectively you come across. Bear in mind that it is illegal to tape both ends of a phone conversation without the other party's approval.

- You likely can improve your success rate by discussing your results with one or two successful salespeople. A skilled telemarketer could be particularly helpful.

- If you don't get through to a contact, hang up and call back the next day.

- Use a script. Run it by several trusted friends for comments. Listen to it on tape until you're comfortable with it. Underline key words in your script to help you learn it quickly and say it more naturally.

Here's an example of a script you can use:

(Your introduction)

"Good morning, Fred. My name is Nancy Tracy. I'm calling to ask for your help. I'm in a career transition. My background is successful experience in high-tech sales, which would be a good fit in the *telecommunications industry.*"

Note: Some people suggest that you ask, "Is this a good time for you to give me a few minutes of your time?" In view of the difficulty of accessing these key people, you're better off going right into your accomplishments, skipping this question. Don't ever ask, "Have I caught you at a bad time?" This question invites rejection.

(Several accomplishments)

"I was able to *increase sales by 37 percent at Barton Industries last year*, so I am now one of their top salespeople. I've cracked several major new accounts, which made up half of the increase."

(Why you're calling)

"I'm calling, Fred, because I'm looking for a new opportunity. I've learned of the excellent reputation of Simplex and its rapid growth, and I am generally familiar with what has brought it about. Are my types of sales skills and achievements things that you would look for in your salespeople?"

(End your introduction with a question to invite a reply.)

If Fred stops you by saying, "I'm just too busy to talk to you now," then:

(Schedule a better time to call)

"Could I get a few minutes of your time *tomorrow*? Would the *morning or afternoon* be better?"

(Use a question to encourage the next step.)

When you call back and reach Fred, your goal is to develop enough interest to get a face-to-face meeting. If this approach fails, turn the conversation into a telephone interview, ending up with:

"Is there *someone else* in the company who might be interested in someone with my background?"

"*What other companies* would you recommend I approach?" Then, "Whom should I talk to?"

BROADCAST LETTER

Exhibit 8-3 is an example of a broadcast letter. This option is practical only if you can get a list of companies that can be downloaded into your computer in an appropriate form so that you can e-mail

EXHIBIT 8-3 • A Broadcast Letter

October 1, 2002

25 Brattle Street
Cambridge, MA 02138

(617) 264-9505

Mr. Ralph Crane
Chief Operations Officer
Forsythe Manufacturing Company
37 Primrose Street
Far Pond, CT 05392

Dear Mr. Crane:

If you're not fully satisfied with the results being generated by your manufacturing operations, I'd like to talk with you about the possibility of my joining your management team.

My achievements as Plant Manager and Quality Manager at two firms include

- The production of over 10 million units without a return
- Productivity increases up to 30%,
- The reduction of over 50% in raw materials inventory
- The reduction of over 60% in injuries and lost days

I achieved these results without significant capital expenditures. In addition, I have supervised up to 125 people, prepared and met budgets, introduced TQM, SPC, and achieved an ISO-9000 Certification.

I have particular expertise involving and empowering employees and have established many teams to focus on quality, maintenance, and safety. I have reduced significantly the bottom line and created a more rewarding workplace for employees.

Before writing you, I gathered information on Forsythe, and I believe you'll find my experience compatible with your situation. I'm confident I can assist you in significantly improving your manufacturing operations.

I will call in a few days. You can also reach me at (617) 264-9505. Thank you for your consideration.

Sincerely,

Deborah Hwang

BACKGROUND: MBA, Albany State University; BA, Economics, University of Rhode Island. Currently working on engineer-in-training certificate. Member, Association for Manufacturing Excellence and the American Society for Quality Control.

your letter to the list. The expense of buying a list or preparing one yourself won't justify the effort. Expect about a 1 percent success rate but only if you have a really good letter. While this response level seems very low, most responses tend to indicate greater promise. In addition, you'll probably get a similar response rate by mailing to the same list three months later.

A broadcast letter can get your background before a large number of decision makers very quickly. If you can get a large list (minimum 500 names, better 1000), it could be a successful strategy for you. Again your best source of help is your support network to obtain a suitable mailing list.

PREPARATION FOR BLIND PROSPECTING

The preparation of your contact list and company research needed are very similar for all three methods.

Get lists of companies from other job hunters, your workshop, and your network. Your next step in preparing the list is to identify the target executive in each company. This is the executive two levels above the job you're seeking. Usually in large companies, he or she would be the Senior Vice President of Marketing and in smaller companies, the CEO. You'll need his or her title, address, and phone number. Obtaining this information could be a considerable chore. Don't reinvent the wheel on this. Many job hunters have learned how to get this information effectively—get the benefit of their advice. Your first choice is to find somebody who'll give you a useful list. Obviously, getting a list that's computerized is essential so that you can input it directly into your computer. If you're trying to reach somebody at the VP or next lower level, the membership list of the local chapter of his or her trade association could be a good source of that information.

A 49-year-old executive used a trade association list for a target letter mailing, and in two months he got 98 prospecting interviews, which uncovered 7 hidden jobs. Useful sources for developing such a list are hoovers.com and Valueline.com. Both charge a fee, but it's modest for a trial.

Your next step is conducting research on each company you're mailing to. Again, hoovers.com and Valueline.com and additionally, finance.yahoo.com are good sources.

It's very important that you compose a very concise and informative letter for either a target letter or broadcast letter. The letter you write can benefit from the work you've done on the PARs and other information in your resume. Get your letter critiqued by a couple of people you have confidence in. Don't shortchange yourself on this review step. Your favorable responses will be very limited even with a good letter; with a poor letter, you may not get any responses.

Bear in mind the experience of John Dinardo who sent out a mailing of a broadcast letter and didn't get a single reply to his first 100 letters. He revised his letter and mailed the new version to 250 CEOs. This time he got 21 offers for interviews. This experience occurred when many job hunters were starting to use PARs a lot in job searches. The success rates are much lower today. Get the advice of several people who have made successful mailings of the type you're planning. Collect successful letter samples.

RECORD KEEPING

Recording the contact list information and tracking the results of target letters, phone prospecting, and broadcast letters is a necessary chore. When you're researching the experience of anyone who has used any of these techniques successfully, ask for their advice also on good ways to organize your records. If you keep haphazard records, you may end up with a real headache.

CHAPTER 9

THE VISIBLE MARKET

The visible market consists primarily of jobs that are being actively recruited for by executive and company recruiters, advertisements, and the Internet. It's the most highly competitive market sector because anyone can apply by merely sending a resume. Thus for a specific recruitment, you're competing against a large pool of candidates. Professional recruiters have developed finely tuned methods of separating viable candidates from the vast majority they have no interest in and whose resumes just clog up their files. When they conduct a search, the recruiters screen the pool for the most promising candidates, and they interview that group, often starting by phone, continually narrowing the field down to a few top choices whom they refer to the senior HR people and the ultimate decision maker for making the final choice.

To contend for jobs in the visible market, candidates must have strong backgrounds with the specialized experience being sought. This chapter shows ways to improve your chances in this visible market. Definitely try the visible market, but if you don't get positive responses, put most of your effort into the hidden market, as described in Chapter 7, "Networking," and Chapter 8, "Blind Prospecting." Many people spend too much time looking in the visible market and have expectations that are unrealistically high.

EXECUTIVE RECRUITERS

Recruiters are engaged by companies seeking professionals at high levels, mostly for key positions in management. Recruiters start by working with the decision maker to define the position the company wants to fill: the functions of the job, its the position in the organization, and the kinds of problems the candidate will face. A key is relevant personality characteristics including those that ensure a compatible fit with the company. Recruiters then write a job description covering all these factors, which they get approved by management.

Then guided by the job description, recruiters develop a pool of candidates from their extensive computer files, their network, advertising, and individual applications. They phone executives holding similar positions to ask for recommendations, often with the possibility that the executive contacted could be a candidate.

Most recruiters have one or two specialties, such as banking or technology, although they do a wide variety of searches. Sometimes they have to work quickly because they're hired after a company has failed in its own search (to avoid the recruiter's fee).

The recruiter's fee is usually about 20 to 30 percent of the annual salary for the executive jobs, somewhat less for lower-level jobs, for which there are more assignments. In general, executive recruiters don't interview unsolicited applicants unless they're candidates for a current assignment or unless they have a strong background in a field the recruiter specializes in.

Occasionally the recruiter specializing in lower-level searches is paid by the successful applicant. When the hiring company doesn't pay, usually it's because it has placed the search request with several recruiters who compete against each other.

Many job hunters have unrealistic expectations of their chances of getting a job through a recruiter. For example, some firms receive more resumes in a day than the number of searches they do in a year.

Sometimes a recruiter can make a good living on only one successful search a month. Ordinarily, a recruiter is working on only a few assignments at any one time.

You contact a recruiter by sending him a letter with your resume, or more likely, e-mailing it. Unless you have strong credentials for the recruiter's typical assignments, your resume gets buried in their filing system. Your best bet to get a recruiter's attention is by a personal introduction that may get some attention for you, but usually the meeting is only a brief courtesy interview. You should accept any opportunity to talk with a recruiter, however, because you may get some useful advice and perhaps even a referral or two.

A recruiter's goal is to place the best candidate in the job because his reputation depends on his number of successful placements. The other major factor in determining his standing in the firm is his ability to attract new business.

THE INTERNET

More and more recruiting activities are conducted via Internet recruiting, using companies like Monster.com. Using the Internet is a useful way of looking for a job, particularly if you have widely sought after skills that are in short supply. Internet recruiting is growing rapidly because it results in a wide range of candidates for a wide range of positions. However, the DBM survey on how people have obtained their jobs shows that only 5 percent found them via the Internet. Nevertheless, this growth will continue. It's absolutely essential in applying for a job via the Internet that your resume scan well. (See Betsy Percival's resume on page 76 for an example of a scannable resume.)

The refinements necessary to be successful using the Internet are changing rapidly. Get advice from job hunters who have used it recently and successfully. Their guidance may be better than a book or article written a year to two ago. You can locate such people through your network, a workshop, perhaps a minicourse, or an Internet chat room.

This advice applies equally to interviewing when you get a positive response to your resume. While the principles of being interviewed via the Internet are similar to those for a face-to-face meeting, the techniques are very different, and they are changing rapidly. Get advice on how to do it effectively from one or two people who have used it effectively.

Top-flight counselors often observe that job hunters spend far too much time applying for jobs via the Internet. Sure, it can be useful for making a reasonable effort for applying to some of its job sites. However, limit your time doing this, unless you're getting some positive replies. It's also obviously very useful for research. Be aware that using the Internet can be addictive. Therefore, develop a discipline by setting specific objectives and a time limit each time you use it.

ANSWERING ADS

The sources of ads for midcareer jobs have diminished. Nevertheless, the best sources are still in use and are the *New York Times*, the *Wall Street Journal*, and your nearest major metropolitan newspaper. However, even these sources usually have considerably fewer ads today than a decade ago. Another useful source is the *National Ad Search Weekly*, which compiles advertised jobs from newspapers and other sources across the country. Particularly promising, it's in some libraries, particularly larger city and college libraries. Its Web site is worth looking at: nationaladsearch.com. It offers a free introductory offer, which you may find worth trying. Exec-U-Net is also a good source of advertised management jobs, for a fee. This company also conducts miniworkshops in major cities. Attend one and see if you think using the service could be useful.

Analyze an ad's requirements carefully. Emphasize your experience that matches these requirements. A letter in which the candidate refers to the job requirements is a welcome relief to a manual screener and is more likely to be selected for the next level of screening. Exhibit 9-1 shows an ad and Exhibit 9-2 a suitable reply. This format is highly recommended because it facilitates the screener's job although it won't help when screening is done by computer, which is happening much more frequently. Sending a resume along with this two-column letter is optional. If you choose to reply with just a conventional letter and resume, at least use a colored pencil to highlight your experience that matches the job's requirements. It's not uncommon for an ad to get 200, 500, or even more replies. The screening process is basically the same as that described for executive recruiters.

Responses to ads are screened initially, when done manually, by a junior HR person whose task is to see how well the resume and letter match a list of requirements. This matching process is quite subject to error because it requires the screener to find and interpret the relevant experience. It's also an assignment that's hard for the screener to concentrate on over the time normally required. The two-column letter may be a welcome relief for the screener and may be more likely to be put in the "for-further-review" pile.

Louis Knowlton, age 61, was experienced in a rapidly growing new specialty. He was turned down when he answered an ad for this specialty from Akron Technology. Undeterred, he identified the probable decision maker. He was correct in his identification of Ted Robbins. Louis called Ted and, without referring to the open job, said, "I am an XYZ specialty engineer between jobs. Could I get 10 minutes of your time?" Ted had waited for two months while HR did its job screening, resulting in only a couple of interviews with unsatisfactory candidates. He was frustrated and so he agreed to see Louis. After 5 minutes, Ted said, "I've read over 200 resumes, and you're better qualified than anyone." Several interviews later, Louis was offered the job. Such aggressiveness can greatly improve your chances of getting the job. It's worth a try. It's an appropriate approach also for any posted jobs you have access to. This approach probably has

EXHIBIT 9-1 • A Typical Recruiting Ad

Industrial Engineer

Leading national consumer products manufacturer located in northwestern Connecticut is seeking a shirt-sleeve type of individual. A BSIE degree and a minimum of 5 years' experience, preferably in a food manufacturing environment. A thorough knowledge of work measurement, plant layout, cost analysis and reduction, and methods of improvement are desired. Salary commensurate with experience. Send resume, including salary history and requirements, in strict confidence to 5943 TIMES.

Exhibit 9-2 • A Reply to the Ad in Exhibit 9-1

Box 5943 TIMES
The New York Times
229 West 43rd Street
New York, NY

RE: Industrial Engineer

Dear Sirs:

In answer to your ad in the May 10 Sunday *Times*, the following highlights of my background show that I am well qualified for the position:

Requirement	*Background*
5 years' experience	7 years' experience
BSIE degree	Rutgers University, New Brunswick, NJ, BSME, 1969
Food manufacturing	Worked for large cosmetic manufacturer for 3 years
Work measurement	Developed time standards for a new packaging line
Plant layout	Assisted in redesign of layout of 100,000-square-foot plant
Cost analysis and reduction	Led a 3-man project team, which developed a program of cost savings and reduction of $400,000 in 6 months
Methods improvement	Assisted in redesigning a toothpaste batching operation to produce 40,000 tubes a day

The attached resume shows other accomplishments pertinent to your Industrial Engineering job. I would like to discuss my background with you in a personal interview.

Yours very truly,

---

a better chance of working if the job has been vacant for a couple of months, but it's worth trying any time.

Many jobs that are advertised for higher-level positions may not be filled for several months, so it is worth sending in a reply even three months after the ad was first run. Sometimes if few candidates are left, you can get more attention at the end of the process as a "fresh face." It's worth going back two or three months in publications that have appropriate ads.

To use this technique you need the name of the company and the Hiring Manager (HM). If they aren't in the ad itself, see if you can learn them through the grapevine. Ask the job hunter's support committee of your trade association. If you know the company name but not the HM's name, participation in a workshop can be useful, where you can tap into members' outreach to expand yours. Otherwise, get the name through the company; try the Operator first, then try Customer Service or Sales.

Time your written answer to an ad carefully. Typically two-thirds of replies to a *Wall Street Journal* ad are received within the first week, so your reply may be looked at more carefully if it arrives in the second week, when there are fewer replies. If the early replies haven't identified a large number of good candidates, the standards may be reduced.

It's often worthwhile to send a second reply in the third week, when even fewer replies are being received. It's unlikely it'll be recognized as a duplicate; but even if it is, it probably doesn't matter. An alternative is sending a letter saying you're disappointed that you haven't received a reply and that you'd like an interview. It's a long shot, but sometimes it works.

JOB FAIRS

Usually a single company or a group of companies holds a job fair to seek lower-level specialists who are in short supply and high demand, such as hospital, technical, biomedical, and computer specialists. Sometimes large companies hold job fairs for many positions, some of which are less specialized. Attending a couple of job fairs can be useful. You may get information on companies that are expanding rapidly.

Your attending may not lead to any job interviews, but it's an opportunity to identify some companies that are expanding, to get background information on them as well as product literature. You'll probably get only a few minutes of the company representative's time unless you have the strong skills they're looking for. Make sure you get his name and phone number so you call him in a couple of days to try to get a longer interview. This may not lead directly to your being seriously considered, but it may provide good background information to prepare a strong target letter to the head of your function in the company. Expanding companies usually have needs in other areas.

Such an event also provides opportunities to network with other attendees. This can be useful in identifying several companies that may have potential needs, sources of help, and so on, and possibly finding a new "buddy."

COLLEGE PLACEMENT OFFICES

Although usually geared to graduating students, frequently college placement offices provide service to alumni and alumnae. They may offer a job matching program and limited career counseling, possibly for a modest fee. They may know of local sources such as useful job hunting libraries. Some maintain a network of graduates who will talk to other graduates. Some distribute a newsletter listing open jobs. An interview with a counselor may help. If you're impressed with him, you may find he freelances for a modest fee; possibly a useful part-time counselor. If your college is not in your local area, try a local college. It may have reciprocal arrangements or may provide useful help anyway.

SECONDARY RECRUITERS

Secondary recruiters are companies that provide some informal recruiting for their clients. Secondary recruiters are banks, law firms, consultants, trade associations and CPA firms. For example, the lending department of a bank may have a few client companies that are looking for a key person so the bank may provide an introduction. Venture capitalists can be particularly useful as they often take a much more active role in their client companies and often advise the management on functional areas that need to be strengthened.

WHEN YOU'RE CONTACTED FOR AN INTERVIEW

An interview with any of these sources can come out of the blue. Think out a game plan for such a call, which may come to you directly or to your assistant who notifies you she's holding a call from someone or a company unknown to you. Do you take the call or defer it until you can return it in private? The caller may want to schedule an interview or is calling to conduct a phone interview to see if you should be invited for a face-to-face interview. If the latter, the two likeliest lines of inquiry are your salary and your experience relative to particular requirements of the job. How to answer the question on salary is dealt with on page 145. If you need privacy or more time to get your thoughts together, ask if you can call the recruiter back.

When you speak to him try to find out the name of the company he's recruiting for, the job title, the name of the interviewer, and the interviewer's title. If you don't get this information, call and ask the recruiter's assistant. Preliminary interviews are with recruiters or with the company's HR people. All are skilled interviewers. They're usually evaluating you for a specific job. If you're interested, the key, as in a job interview, is making as favorable an impression as possible to get a personal interview. Make sure also to get the name of the company so you can do research on it before the interview.

It has already been emphasized that making a favorable impression is a key to success in dealing with both the hidden and visible markets. Let's now look at some things you can do to become a better salesman of yourself in order to do this.

CHAPTER 10

"JOB HUNTING IS SELLING YOURSELF"

SELLING YOURSELF IS A KEY

The statement is one of several half-truths you often hear about job hunting. It refers to winning favor for yourself in the eyes of others to make them feel and believe you have strong experience and will make an excellent employee in the right position. People who have particularly persuasive communications skills have an advantage over many job hunters. Gaining proficiency in persuasion is useful not only for your job hunt but also in your future career. Selling yourself does not rely on gimmicks but rather on proven sales techniques. This chapter describes techniques used successfully in sales training programs.

FOCUS ON IMPROVING YOUR SELLING SKILLS

Some job hunters are unaware that they're not getting themselves across effectively, despite their intelligence and good experience. If you are concerned about your presentation, invite criticism, as described on page 105, and take advantage of the information you receive.

Many job hunters with successful careers may have worked on jobs in which they interacted with the same relatively small group of people day after day. If so, they may have been able to get along with only passable communications skills. In a job search, however, a weak presentation considerably limits your opportunities and will lead to a longer search with a less satisfactory result. If your selling skills are only passable, be comforted in knowing you have plenty of company, including lots of successful job hunters. However, use this opportunity to become a better salesman of yourself to help in your job search and in the future.

This chapter has two purposes: to increase awareness of this important yet often overlooked aspect of job hunting and to teach you some simple techniques.

Selling in a job search is different from the selling you're used to in other roles, in several ways:

- You're trying to get the interest and support of a different person in every interview—sometimes someone you know, most often someone you don't know.
- You're selling a single product: yourself.
- You get only one opportunity to sell to each person, unlike a salesman who's selling a product or service often to repeat customers.
- You're trying to make one, very big sale, one of the most important sales of your life.
- You are basically delivering the same message day after day to various people. Although this repetition can be frustrating, it works to your advantage because you can become more skilled at the various aspects of interviewing than the people you interview with. Most of what occurs in a networking or job interview has occurred in your previous interview experience, so you can prepare for it.
- Your goal is to succeed at each job interview, so you can move to the next step, and the next, until you get an offer.

+ You will learn from every interview. You'll be able to improve your skill in dealing with unexpected issues and prepare answers for the next time these issues come up.

Here are some specific techniques that may be useful.

Monitoring Your Demeanor

Learn to deal with the feeling of being out of the loop. All job hunters feel this this way to some extent. The best antidote is to keep a full calendar and to continually improve getting yourself across.

Be an intelligent listener and a brief talker. Let the interviewer do two-thirds of the talking. A senior vice president of one of the largest executive recruiting firms in the country sits in on most first interviews between a client and a candidate. He has noticed that most employers are turned off by candidates who do most of the talking. Conversely, he has noticed that many interviewers are favorably impressed by candidates who let the interviewers do most of the talking. Sometimes an interviewer says, "I was impressed by this candidate, although I admit I have quite a few unanswered questions about her."

In an interview, always conduct yourself as if you're interested. Don't lounge in your chair. Sit on the front of it, and lean forward to project interest and alertness.

Look the interviewer straight in the eye fairly frequently. Try not to act wooden.

Smile, because you'll come across in a less perfunctory and more human way, even on the phone.

Leave a voice mail message with a friend or two, and ask them what their reaction to your message is.

Use "sales improvement" tapes or CDs. It's easy to listen to them in your car.

Be businesslike—friendly and reasonably relaxed.

Observe the interviewer's body language. Does the interviewer seem bored? Are you getting the person's full attention? If it not, work on establishing rapport with the interviewer.

Really listen, not just to what she says but to what you think she means.

Don't focus on what you want to say so much that you don't listen to what the interviewer says.

Use the pronouns *you* and *your* frequently.

When you talk on the phone, stand up because you'll come across more forcefully.

When you talk on the phone, also look in the mirror occasionally. The image you see reflects the tone that the receiver hears. Here again smiling projects a better image.

Invite criticism on your communication skills in interviews when appropriate.

Almost every day, we all are exposed to how poorly intelligent people communicate by what we frequently hear on voice mail. All of us get a lot of voice mail and answering machine messages with people on the other end rattling off phone numbers so fast you have to listen to the message several times to understand it. Some of the common mistakes are that they're speaking too loudly or too softly, too fast, or not pronouncing a difficult personal or company name that they should spell.

Practice leaving messages on voice mail:

• Tape several messages and critique them.

• Get someone to listen to the tape to also critique it.

• Are your statements the right length?

• Are you clear and positive?

• Do you have pauses, "ers," "you know," etc.?

+ If your name is unusual, pronounce it clearly and spell it
  if necessary.

+ Say phone numbers slowly and repeat them.

If you have a heavy accent, make sure you are being understood. Talk slowly and make sure you're speaking loudly enough. Ask for some honest feedback. Once you've gotten your new job, you should think of overcoming this problem by joining something like Toastmasters, taking accent modification training, etc. Too strong an accent could be a real obstacle in your future career.

SOME SELLING TECHNIQUES

Discuss selling techniques with several friends, particularly those who are effective salespeople. Their advice can be useful on such things as the following:

+ Getting appointments

+ Dealing with obstacles, rejections, and roadblocks

+ Calling someone on the telephone, including interviewing on
  the telephone

+ Getting the interviewer more involved

These people have shown by their success that they can deal with these problems. They undoubtedly can give you some useful tips on this important aspect of job hunting.

Keep in mind that you're a product that's being sold. There are two ways of doing this: selling benefits (your accomplishments) and features (your skills). Your PARs, are most effective in getting the interviewer to understand what you can do and to paint him a picture that he can visualize and remember. Describing your skills is good for summarizing, such as in Your Two-Minute Introduction (page 142).

If a couple of your outstanding achievements are consistently getting weak reactions from interviewers, you're probably describing them ineffectively. Sam Page got weak reactions whenever he described his outstanding achievement. On his way to an important interview with Carole MacAllister, he decided to describe this experience differently—in this case, in more detail. Several years later, he recalled her exact reply: "That shows you're really smart and highly motivated." Sam realized he had been shortchanging himself by thinking interviewers would understand his brief description of this achievement and be impressed. This incident emphasizes the importance of *experimenting*, particularly in low-risk situations such as networking interviews, until you get fairly consistent positive reactions from your interviewers.

Through networking and your research, find the resources that could be particularly useful to someone like you in improving your selling skills: specific individuals, workshops, networking groups, or Internet sources. Volunteer counselors and former job hunters can be particularly helpul in this.

Write out answers to questions you're likely to be asked. Prepare for likely criticisms and roadblocks. Discuss your answers and strategies with a trusted friend.

Here are some strategies for answering questions effectively:

1. Listen to the question. Be sure you understand it. Ask for clarification if necessary, conveying that you're really listening and that you feel that the question is really important. Occasionally repeat the question to show, again, that you're really listening.

2. Take enough time to think through your answer. Most interviewers are glad when you don't wing it.

3. Use only positive information. Be complete, but try not to open areas of difficulty. Be truthful.

4. Prepare answers to typical questions. Turn an awkward question to your advantage.

Develop several ways of answering questions. For example, rephrase the question in more favorable terms. If asked, "Were you fired?" rephrase it as, "Why did I leave XYZ?" You haven't admitted to being fired, and you have given yourself more latitude in phrasing the answer. You'll recognize this technique as one used frequently by politicians.

Prepare a sequence of answers for difficult or sensitive questions. If asked, "Why did you leave XYZ?" your first answer might be, "I was ready to move on to a new position," or "When Jack Smith took over as sales manager, four of his seven department heads left within a year." Then stop. Only if the interviewer demands more information should you give your second answer: "My boss and I differed philosophically as to where we were trying to take the operation." Stop again. Often the issue won't be pursued further. Only if you're directly asked again should you give your third answer: "I was let go because the boss wanted his own man." With the volatility of the job market in the last few years, how you left your last job is usually of much less importance than it used to be.

Answer the question with another question. For example, "Aren't you overqualified?" "What makes you think I'm overqualified?"

Take the offensive by turning an apparent liability into an asset. "Why didn't you go to college?" "I'm self-educated. I have competed continually with college-educated people and I have more than held my own."

Answer a question with a statement that could be viewed as a strength rather than a weakness. "What's your greatest weakness?" "Some people say I'm a workaholic."

Acknowledge the statement and then rebut it (the "yes, but" answer): "It's true that I don't have networking experience, but I didn't have software experience before I went to XYZ. In a matter of six months, I was able to straighten out a messed up development operation that they had been working on for over a year. In fact, one of the things I'm proudest of is my ability to handle successfully assignments for which I don't have the necessary experience. I view them as an opportunity to broaden my skills."

Sometimes the best answer is, "I don't know."

Just as you're about to go into an interview, repeat to yourself, "This is going to be the best interview I've ever had." A little bit of pumping yourself up gets your energy up.

Experiment with using your PARs, answering questions, and dealing with roadblocks in low-risk networking interviews. You may find a more detailed answer to a particular question may get a more positive response than you've been getting.

If a problem comes up in an interview, visualize how a hotshot salesman (call him Chip) would have handled it. The Chips of this world come up with creative ways to overcome sticky situations. Visualizing a creative and confident approach may help you handle similar situations in the future.

"No" doesn't necessarily mean "no." To Chip, "no" is like waving a flag in front of a bull. He'll often find a way to turn it around to "yes."

Avoid controversial subjects. If the interviewer brings them up, steer the conversation back to something neutral as soon as you can. Don't be argumentative, but don't always agree. Either extreme is a sign of weakness. If you disagree, say so, tactfully: "Yes, I see your point, but . . . ," then make your point.

If the interview is interrupted, pick up where the conversation left off. If the interviewer doesn't want to pursue the same subject, ask, "Would you like to hear about my experience in X or in Y?" Find out what the interviewer is most interested in.

Don't expect every interview to be successful. This doesn't happen. Babe Ruth is remembered for his long-standing record of 60 home runs in one season. For a long time, however, he also held the record for the most strike-outs in a career!

Take samples of your work, if appropriate. For example, a marketing plan or a major report show the depth of your thinking and your organizing ability. (But make sure you don't breach confidentiality.)

DEALING WITH REJECTION

A key part of successful interviews is dealing with rejection:

* You probably don't have the skill of Chip, who is undoubtedly an expert in dealing with rejection, so work on improving this skill.

* Don't take rebuffs personally; they're just part of the process.

* Remember the easiest thing for an interviewer to say is no. He or she will say no if he or she has any doubts. Don't accept it, keep the conversation going. Ask a question, or "May I make another point?" As long as there's a dialogue, there's a chance. *"No" doesn't mean "no." It means you haven't convinced the interviewer.*

* Probe for the real reason you were rejected. Often the first reason isn't the real reason. Ask "Why?" or "Would you expand on that?"

* If you feel you're being judged unfavorably against an interviewer's hidden agenda, take the offensive. Initiate the subject even if it's illegal for the interviewer to bring it up. Such a hidden agenda may be age, lack of specific experience, or ability for a man to work for a woman or for a much younger person. For example, if age is the issue, describe your experience of working well with a younger boss, your record of being accepted by junior people who regularly have sought your advice, and how younger employees ask you to socialize with them. Emphasize your recent work with long hours under pressure, demonstrate that your skills are state of the art, or specify that you're an active person in an athletic or fitness program.

- Promote yourself. No one else is going to do it for you. Saying that you want the job, that you're confident you can do it well, and that you will deliver from the day you step on board may get you the offer.

You probably won't need all of these techniques. Using some of them, however, can help your search. Don't expect these techniques to be successful the first time you use them. Practice them, and experiment with them, until they're effective for you. They won't only help you in your job search, but they'll make you more effective in the rest of your career.

CHAPTER 11

PREPARING FOR INTERVIEWS

So far, you've done overall preparation for your job search. Now get ready to apply all this work to job interviews. This is the time to pull everything together including the research you'll do on the company so that you can put your best foot forward.

The key things an interviewer is trying to learn about you are your skills in dealing with the principal problems of the job and do you have the personal characteristics needed to be successful in the position (your drive, motivation, communications skills, determination, reliability, listening skills, analytical skills, ability to fit in and lead others, to name a few).

Your most useful tools are your expanded PARs. Take a few minutes every couple of weeks to make sure you're using them most effectively in your interviews. If you find that one or two don't seem to elicit the desired response, try varying how you present them.

Review Chapter 10, "Job Hunting Is Selling Yourself." Particularly focus on the three or four most important items for you.

Typically, interviewers start an interview by saying, "Tell me about yourself." If the interviewer does not give you that opening, then volunteer, "Perhaps you'd like to hear something about me." This is an opportunity for you to give your Two-Minute Introduction. Here's an example.

The Two-Minute Introduction

I went to Wesleyan and then worked for three years for Trainor Securities on Wall Street. I got my MBA in 1995 from Albany Business School. I joined Montgomery Plastics in Cleveland, where I was Assistant Controller for a company with about 3000 employees. Two years later, I was made Controller, and five years later, Chief Financial Officer. I held this role until we were bought out by Bailor Industries several months ago.

My background in finance involves a wide variety of activities, including arranging a $25 million IPO, overseeing the financial planning process and all the accounting and bank relations. While I was at Montgomery, the company grew at the rate of about 17 percent a year, with last year's sales close to $70 million and profits of $3.5 million. I am known as a hands-on individual, a developer of strong people, a team player coming up with creative solutions, and someone with great determination.

That's an overview of my career. At the outset, I want you to know I'm here to help you find out what you may want to find out about me.

Tape it and listen to it. Is it clear? Get it critiqued. Don't memorize it; just familiarize yourself with the flow of it.

RESEARCHING THE COMPANY

There are a lot of sources of information on public companies. One of the best sites is hoovers.com, which provides on each company some financial information, names of key executives, and product information, as well as company news and competitors' names. Some of it is free, but the best is usually available for a fee, which is modest for a month's trial. A free site is finance.yahoo.com, which provides a lot of financial information and often one or more investment analyst reports, which are particularly useful in identifying company problems. Another good source is Valueline.com, which provides for a fee a very valuable one-page summary of the company's finances, operations, and major problems. Many libraries subscribe to Valueline reports in printed document form. SEC extensive financial and operational reports are available at sec.gov/edgarhp.htm. Stockbrokers often can also furnish useful information on these companies.

For many private companies, hoovers.com is also useful, although obviously financial information isn't included. The best source of information on these companies, which is also available for public companies, is their Web sites. Also before an interview, call the company's public relations or advertising departments and ask them to send to the receptionist such information as newspaper articles about the company, news releases, a product catalog, or speeches by the CEO or other prominent executives—any of which you can read by arriving early for your interview. Bankers, lawyers, accountants, suppliers, salespersons, and competitors can also furnish company information. Often such information is available in the waiting room. Other useful sources of information on the industry are trade publications—try your chosen publication name.com because many of them are on the Internet.

RESEARCH ON THE INTERVIEWER

The most difficult kind of information to get is about the interviewer. Get his name and title when you set up the interview. Make sure you know how to spell and pronounce his name. Look on the company Web site for this kind of information. Some have biographies of the principal officers. Use your network, a workshop network, a competitor, or a trade association to find out how long he has been with the company, his professional reputation, his rough age, and community activities he may be involved in. Ask public relations or advertising to send a copy of his or her biography to the receptionist.

Other useful sources are your banker, accountant, lawyer, or prominent trade association, which can often give you information about the company and its prospects and problems. A competitor can give you some insight on what's going on in the industry. Salespeople who call on a company can be another source of useful information about it.

YOUR REFERENCES

Hiring companies use references differently. Some ignore them while others pursue them carefully. Companies usually have all requests for references referred to HR these days because of possible legal ramifications. HR ordinarily will give out only your title, the years you worked there, and sometimes your salary, so ask coworkers to give you a favorable reference. Poor references can hurt you; good ones may help. Even a poor reference, though, can often be defused.

If you're forced to use someone who'll give you a bad reference, such as your last boss, tell the interviewer that this reference will probably be unfavorable and explain why. Name several coworkers who will give you a good reference and often explain why your boss is giving you a bad reference.

Call all your references and get their permission before you use them. Take to each interview a list of your references, including the person's name, title, address, and phone number. In today's turmoil, references have moved or changed functions, so the inquiry may be passed on to someone who knows little about you. If you're likely to get a reference from such a third party, ask a friend to verify the kind of reference you'll get. If a particularly useful reference has moved, try to find a current address through a mutual friend or the real estate agent who sold the person's house. Finally, inform a reference about a particular job you're being considered for so that the reference can make a more intelligent report about you. Protect your relationship with your references by giving out their names only when there's a valid reason.

Every month or so, call your references to update them on your progress.

BE READY FOR TOUGH QUESTIONS

Generally, recruiters and hiring executives ask different types of questions. The Hiring Manager is focused on the job, how well the candidate's skills and experience match the job's requirements, and how well the candidate is likely to fit into the company. Recruiters are more interested in a candidate's work history and his personal characteristics.

Here are some typical questions asked by the hiring managers and others asked by recruiters. Select about 10 in each group, and write out rough answers. Don't memorize the answers. Tape your answers and listen to them to make sure that you're responding to the questions clearly and confidently. Test your answers on a friend. Ask him to listen to your taped answers and critique them. If you run into a key question you're not prepared for, add it to your list. Review strategies for answering questions on pages 136 through 138 to make yourself more effective in answering them.

Questions from the Hiring Manager

Salary. This is a key issue that must be handled skillfully. Be well prepared with a good estimate of what the probable ballpark figure is of the salary for the position you're seeking. Research it with one or two friendly recruiters and/or members of your trade association job support committee or your network. The salary question comes up in many forms such as, What was your last salary? What has been your salary history? What is your salary expectation? However worded, the inquiry is basically the same. If it occurs early in the interview, try to delay answering it by saying something like, "Salary is important, but can we defer discussing it until I know more about your job requirements?" Ultimately, you have to address it. Probably your best approach is stating $95,000 (the actual figure) but adding, if true, "I've been getting annual raises, and I was due for another one in two months." Another answer, though it can be risky, is "My goal is $105,000." Try to avoid being trapped into naming a figure that is too low because that's likely to be the ceiling that will be considered. Other approaches are described on page 188.

Job Requirements. Most of the questions will be about specific requirements of the job and your related experiences. Some are apt to be about your universal skills such as completing assignments on time, within budget, and your relationship with others in your prior companies. Others may be the following:

- Why did you leave your last job?
- What do you think you would bring to the company?
- Based on what you know about this job, what changes would you make?
- How do you keep yourself up to date with the new technology?
- What are the three things that motivate you most?
- How long do you think it will be before you'll be effective here, in a different industry?
- Have you ever had to do a job without having the needed experience?
- You've changed jobs twice in the last four years. How long are you likely to stay with us?
- Give me a couple of examples of how you successfully worked under pressure.
- What do you view as the ideal relationship with your boss?

Questions from HR and Recruiters

- What would you change about yourself?
- What were your biggest failures?

- How well would you work for a younger person?
- How well would you work for a woman?
- What did you dislike most about your last job?
- If you were starting out now, what would you do differently?
- What three things have you done that you're most proud of?
- What kind of criticism have you received?
- Was it deserved? What did you do about it?
- Have you ever failed at an assignment? Why?

Questions to Ask Hiring Managers

- Is the organization plan to offset ABC's entry into high-resolution TV paying off well? [Note this question shows you've done research on the company.]
- What has caused MNO's [a competitor] stock price to drop off so much in the last month compared with the industry? [Another question showing you've done research.]
- What are one or two things you'd like to see accomplished in this job in the next three months?
- What changes would you like to see in your operation in the next two years?
- What do you see as the key factors for success on this job?
- Does anyone in your department feel entitled to this position?
- How will you evaluate the new hire in about six months?
- Why is the position open?
- How long was the predecessor in the position?
- What happened to his predecessor? [If there have been several people on the job in a short period, beware, it may be the boss is a tough person to work for.]

PRACTICE LISTENING AND INTERVIEWING

Often job hunters miss important information the interviewer conveys. You can sharpen your listening skill by tape recording and listening to dialogue from the radio or TV. Record 5 minutes of dialogue as you're listening. Then write down all you heard. Compare it with the actual recording. Then do it for 10 minutes. Do this exercise several times until you've sharpened your listening skills—so you won't be missing key points people are making in interviews.

Ask a friend to conduct a mock interview with you while it's being recorded on a video. View the results paying particular attention to your posture, eye contact, how you answer the questions (the pace, the clarity of your answers), tone, and upsetting mannerisms. Ask your friend to critique your performance.

LEARNING FROM INTERVIEWS

On page 158, you'll be introduced to making a postinterview analysis after every interview. Add any key things you learned in an interview to *Your Interview Checklist*. You should glance over it before every interview. Keep it manageable—say, five to six items. When you add another item, delete any you've got under control.

CHAPTER 12

IMPROVING YOUR INTERVIEWING EFFECTIVENESS

PERSPECTIVE

You've been invited for an actual job interview. Now you have an opportunity to use all your preparation and hard work to convince an employer of your strong experience. Make sure you're carefully prepared:

+ Carefully research the company and, if possible, the Hiring Manager.

+ Review your PAR list, within the last two weeks.

+ Review your interview checklist.

+ Make a "failure analysis" (page 171) on the upcoming interview, visualizing the principal things that could go wrong and how you'll cope with them.

+ Go over your list of tough questions and your answers.

+ Say to yourself, to become pumped up, "This is going to be my best interview ever."

An interview runs from when you first meet the receptionist until you leave the building. A misstep with anybody, even the receptionist, can hurt you. The Hiring Manager is eager to hire somebody as soon as possible, which works to your advantage. Interviewing is time-consuming on top of all the other demands of his or her job. Furthermore, the position needs to be filled for the manager to get the necessary work done.

As the candidate, your objectives in the interview are the following:

- convince the Hiring Manager that you're the best candidate.
- assess whether this job is the best one you're likely to find.

The objectives of the interviewer are to determine whether

- you have the experience, skills, and personality needed.
- you're likely to be the most effective of all the candidates for the position.
- you're likely to be a good fit with the rest of the company.
- If you're the best candidate, can you be persuaded to take the job?

THE INTERVIEW

Arrive at least 10 minutes early, so you can take time to observe the general atmosphere of the outer office and review your notes again. Dress the way you would dress for doing that job. If in doubt, err on the side of being conservative. Notice the condition and layout of the office, how people are dressed, and how they relate to each other. If there's a delay, stay relaxed about it and observe. In the chit-chat with the Hiring Manager's assistant, try to find out how long the interview is likely to last so that you can make sure you'll be able to address your key issues.

The Introduction

Greet the interviewer with a smile and a firm handshake. Try to select a chair where you can easily sit upright and where you don't have glaring light or the sun in your face. Engage in a few minutes of pleasantries—about the weather, the traffic, or some topical event. Observe the interviewer's office. Is the desk neat or cluttered? Do the pictures on the wall indicate a hobby? How is the interviewer dressed?

Expect at the start a question like, "Tell me a little about yourself." This opens the door for your Two-Minute Introduction, which you were shown how to prepare on page 142. If you aren't asked this question, volunteer, "Would you like me to tell you a little bit about myself?" At the end of this introduction, you might say something like, "My objective is to help you find out all you want to know about me. How would you like to proceed?" The interviewer will probably ask you a question about your background or tell you something about the company and the job. Either way, as soon as you can, get the Hiring Manager to talk about the job and its requirements. Bear in mind the interviewer usually forms a pretty definite impression of you in the first 10 minutes.

Your Work Experience

This phase of the interview makes up most of it. It involves the interviewer asking a series of questions usually requesting you to describe various phases of your experience related to the job.

Your key tool for describing your experiences is using your expanded PARs related to each question. If the interviewer asks for more detail, it indicates that he or she is interested in this aspect of your experience. If you don't get a positive response to several of your PARs, experiment, perhaps being more detailed, in each description.

The following questions will help keep the focus on the interviewer's agenda:

+ "What other experience is of particular interest?"

+ "Would you rather hear about X or Y?"

Let the interviewer do about two-thirds of the talking.

Your objective in the first interview is to get a second interview. Your objective thereafter is to get the next interview, and the next, until you get an offer. If you've been looking for some time, it's worthwhile to get an offer even if you don't accept it. The offer boosts your morale. You may even be able to upgrade the offer to one that is suitable.

Focus on your prospective boss. Identify three to five traits. Remember you're probably seeing this person's best behavior. Any adverse traits you observe are unlikely to improve. Be also sensitive to his or her body language.

Observe the people you meet and the surroundings. Observe how they interact. Is the atmosphere tense or sloppy, friendly or businesslike?

Probe for the interviewer's hangups, such as getting a job done on time, expecting to be kept informed on everything, or being a stickler for detail.

During the interview, observe the behavior of the interviewer. If the interviewer is passive or uninterested in you, change your approach.

Show you're really interested:

+ Frequently look right into the eyes of the interviewer.
+ Smile occasionally.
+ Sit on the front edge of your chair and lean forward.
+ Once in a while, ask the interviewer to repeat the question (this shows you feel what the interviewer is saying is important).
+ Similarly, say "Let me see if I understand this correctly," and then repeat what the interviewer has said.
+ Take notes.

As the interview progresses, ask some of the following questions:

+ "What are the two or three most important things you're looking for in a candidate?"

+ "Why is the position open?"
+ "What do you expect the new hire to achieve in the first six months?"
+ "How will you evaluate my performance at the end of six months?"
+ "What changes would you expect within two years?"
+ "What are likely to be the first couple of assignments?"
+ "What did the last person in this position do well? Not so well?"
+ "How long had that person been on the job? If a short time, why did the predecessor leave?" (If the last two people both left after a short time, beware.)

Sometimes a key item is a hidden issue. For someone in midcareer, it might be age, which is an issue the interviewer cannot legally raise but an issue nonetheless that could be held against you. It's important for you to raise the issue to defuse it:

"I had a good relationship with my boss at Harris Spring. He was 11 years younger than I am. He had a lot of new ideas and was willing to take considerable risks. I think he valued my judgment as he often used me as a sounding board. He often then modified his plans to prevent them from going awry."

"I play for my club in a tennis league and still downhill ski a lot."

"The last couple of years have been the most exciting of my career. I have accomplished more, worked under greater pressure, and done more on-the-job traveling than at any other time during my career."

Don't say you can solve the employer's problems. A lot of work may have been done on a particular problem, so saying you can solve it easily would be a turnoff. Say you'd study the situation carefully, including what has already been done and the principal obstacles. Point out you've faced similar problems and have used such-and-such an approach that accomplished the objective, but stress that any solution you attempted in the new position would be tailor-made for your new company.

An issue that comes up quite frequently is a perceived lack of experience in one of the requirements of the job. You should admit that you don't have that exact experience but then describe your most comparable experience. Then end up your answer with a statement such as, "I've always prided myself on my ability to successfully tackle problems where I didn't have the required experience. For example, with little experience in coordinating with issues between engineering and manufacturing, at Merrill I was asked to straighten out a flawed design of our LM line, which was having over 40percent rejections. With an engineer I was able to get two design changes made, and then I got manufacturing to make the proper production changes so that within a month rejections were reduced to less than 5 percent."

When Ken Murray, the Hiring Manager, raises the subject of salary, try to defer the discussion until after there's been a good give-and-take on the requirements of the job. If you, Anne Carson, the candidate, are pressed on the subject, suggest that it will depend on the job requirements so it should be discussed later. The best strategy for revealing your most recent salary is on page 145. The issue of negotiating salary is discussed on page 187.

The Wind-up

How you handle the closing may improve your chances of getting an offer or to the next round of interviews.

Franny Gillespie was a candidate for a major CFO job. At the end of her interview, she asked, "Where do we have a fit, and where don't we have a fit"? Fred MacMahon, the Hiring Manager, said to Franny, "I don't think you're aggressive enough." She replied, "I can see how you might have gotten that impression. I'd like to describe an experience I think might change your opinion." She then went on to relate an important accomplishment that showed she could be very aggressive. After this exchange, the interview continued another three hours. When it was ending, the interviewer said, "You'll certainly be on my list of three final candidates."

Fight for yourself because nobody else is going to do it for you. If you don't get a commitment, ask, "What's the next step?" You may discover how many candidates are being considered, how many are likely to be brought back for the next round, and the timing.

Here are some ideas for closing an interview:

- "Based on my understanding of the job requirements, I'm confident I can do a first-class job for you. What do you think?" Asking for a reaction may be enough to get to the next step or even to get an offer. Asking for a commitment increases the chances of getting one.

- "As we're wrapping up, I'd like to review what we've talked about. It seems to me that you're looking for somebody with strong experience developing markets and introducing complex new services. My experience at Blair Industries shows a strong record in both of these. Finally, I'd just like to say that, if you decide to offer me the job, I will do everything I can to make you feel you've made a good decision."

- "Mary, I would just like to thank you for your consideration and for the time you've spent with me. It would be useful to me if you could tell me why I'm not being chosen for the position. I'm eager for your frank assessment."

Another closing to an unsatisfactory interview might be, "Now I understand how you arrived at your decision. I'm afraid I'm pretty rusty on interviewing; I haven't done it for eight years. I am impressed with the position, and I feel I'm capable of doing a top-notch job for you. I really feel I'm capable of coming across much better to you than I did today. I guess all of us have our bad days. I'd like another chance to show you why my experience and skills make me a strong candidate. Can we set up a time?" Here, you have nothing to lose, but you may be able to save the current situation. At least, you may learn something that will improve your interviewing in the future.

If the interview fails, thank the interviewer sincerely and ask for some candid criticism. Also ask if he has any thoughts on what companies would be good for you to approach. You just might learn something that's valuable.

Realize that failure happens to all job hunters at some time. Accept it; don't beat up yourself over it. Just learn what you can from it.

Other People in the Company

A conversation with the Hiring Manager's peers is usually less formal than the interview itself. The Hiring Manager is trying to portray the job in a good light and present herself as a good boss to work for. Her peer is likely to be more candid about problems with the job. For example, ask why the previous employee left. Was it because of the boss's unrealistic expectations, poor direction, or inadequate resources? Any of these reasons can mean a "yellow light." Probe the situation discreetly with the peer. You may get a very different slant than you did from the Hiring Manager.

Meeting the boss's boss gives you another picture that could affirm or contradict what you've learned to date.

Be friendly with the interviewer's assistant, who can provide important information after the interview, such as the names, the spelling, and the titles of the people you've met. Find a common interest or two. An assistant who's favorably disposed toward you may give you a progress report on the hiring process when you ask him, sometimes even subtly boost your standing.

POSTINTERVIEW ACTIVITIES

Analyzing and reflecting on any job interview should make you better prepared for future ones. Because you're likely to get only a few actual job interviews, make the most of any you get. Right after an interview, reflect on what went on for 10 minutes. Record the key issues that came up. Fill out the "Postinterview Analysis," Exhibit 12-1, which helps you improve the impression you make through followup so you will be better prepared for the next interview.

The Thank-You Letter

The next day, send a typed thank-you letter to the principal interviewer (Exhibit 12-2). This letter is another opportunity to sell yourself, though its main purpose is to express appreciation for the interview. Some feel a handwritten letter is acceptable. An e-mail isn't as good, though it's fine for the other people you talked to. Drop the Hiring Manager's assistant a thank-you note (most applicants won't bother, so it will help to be remembered favorably).

Over the next week, do further research on American Foods with the hope that you will be granted the next interview. Focus your research on things you learned in your first interview. Through your network, try to identify a few people who know American Foods so you can chat with them on the phone to find out about its operations in your field. Look for people who are former employees of the company or suppliers or buyers of the product to give you information.

Improving the Impression You Left

A week or so before you estimate that the interviewer is making the final choice of candidates for the next round, send him an *upon-further-reflection letter*, Exhibit 12-3. This letter reaffirms your credentials relating to the company's most pressing needs, defuses any reservations the interviewer might have, and contains pertinent information

EXHIBIT 12-1 • Postinterview Analysis

Company _____

_____

_____

Date_____ Length of interview_____

Interviewer _____(name, nickname, title, personality traits, interests)

Other people met_____

Summarize important things the interviewer said (advice, criticism, names, problems, plans, job requirements, "hot buttons," sensitive areas, closing remarks). Be specific.

Summarize things you said that got strongly positive or negative reactions (opening remarks, points emphasized, sensitive areas, etc.).

"Things you wish you'd said." (Include them in the thank-you letter.)

What are the principal requirements of the job? (What problems would you be expected to solve? What's the yardstick for measuring performance?)

How was the interview concluded?

What are the interviewer's reservations about you?

What was your perception of the interviewer? (Describe three to five traits.)

What can you do now to improve your impression (e.g., answer questions raised or make useful suggestions) Perhaps you can send an article of particular interest.

Exhibit 12-1 • Postinterview Analysis *(continued)*

Who (if anybody) should you inform about the interview (recruiter, referrer, etc.)?

Include in your followup letter corrections, additions, research, reminders.

Did you ask to be part of the next step? If you were rejected, why? Did you fight to get reconsidered?

Did you get referrals if interview didn't work out?

If the interview was a result of a referral from a third party, should you get feedback from the third party?

Rate your interview performance, on a scale of 10 (high) to 1 (low)?

What could you have done to make the grade higher?

If you could do the interview over again, knowing what you know now, what would you do differently?

In preparation?

In the interview?

Should you add anything to your interview preparation checklist?

EXHIBIT 12-2 • Thank-You Letter Sent Immediately after a First Interview

<table>
<tr><td></td><td>January 10, 2004</td></tr>
</table>

Mr. Frank Joyce
Chief Financial Officer
American Foods Company
735 Seventh Avenue
New York, NY 10918

Dear Mr. Joyce:

Thank you

It was a pleasure to talk with you Monday afternoon. The position of Controller is a wonderful opportunity for me to apply the financial control experience I gained for five years at Superior Biscuit as Assistant Controller.

I understand the importance you place on standardizing the controls and financial reporting system of the three plants of Peerless you recently acquired. Also I can understand the need for speeding up your monthly statements from four to two days.

Review of highlights

I was in charge of the financial aspects of Superior Biscuit's three acquisitions in seven years, and I have dealt with both these problems. I oversaw change in the acquired companies' financial systems and controls to conform to ours. I'm known as someone who can win cooperation and realize good results quickly.

Your capabilities related to the interviewer's needs

In conclusion, I feel I'm well qualified for the position and am very interested in it. I developed a reputation for consistently exceeding expectations in my work. I look forward to hearing from you next week about another chance to get together. If I don't hear from you by the 15th, I will call to see where matters stand.

I appreciate your time and interest.

Sincerely,

Ask for action

you learned from your research. Because this letter is unusual, you may stand out enough to get to the next round of interviews.

INTERVIEW TIPS

Dress in a style you think is appropriate for the job you're applying for. If in doubt, err on the conservative side. Follow any specific instructions from the person arranging the interview. Be well groomed.

When you're asked a question, provide the best answer to what you think is being looked for. Then stop. Don't add things that are possibly irrelevant or could raise problems.

EXHIBIT 12-3 • Upon-Further-Reflection Letter

January 30, 2004

Mr. George Smith
Vice President of Sales
Federal Transformer Company
637 Grand Avenue
Cleveland, OH 20704

Dear Mr. Smith:

Recall of interview	The more I think of the position of Sales Manager of Federal, the more I am excited by it. Not only do I think it is a wonderful opportunity, but I feel that it represents the kind of long-term challenge I'm looking for. Your company's goals and the organizational chemistry that I perceived particularly impressed me.
The company's needs, your capabilities	My 17 years in sales and sales management, mostly in the electrical industry, provide me with considerable problem-solving experience that should be very useful to the Federal sales effort. I took over Acme Control's Sales Manager's position 4 years ago in a downturn similar to what Federal is now experiencing. My first year and a half there I was able to strengthen the sales team so that Acme experienced only a 9% decrease in sales as compared to over 21% average for its three major competitors. I revised the sales incentive plan and greatly increased the training and upgrading of our requirements for new sales staff. These elements were major factors in this success.

That I was able to have this effect at Acme indicates I was able to size up what was needed and could develop and execute a plan quickly. This success wasn't at the expense of future progress because considerable improvement was made over the next several years. My emphasis on a team approach reduced sales staff turnover by 55% in the first two years.

New information	I don't recall mentioning a followup and control system I developed to increase the number of new accounts considerably. I also engineered new uses for our transformers at Acme in the paper industry, which enabled us to make substantial inroads in this industry for the first time.
Left in question	You will recall we discussed the possibility of distributing your equipment on a lease basis. I have since learned that two of the large machine tool manufacturers (Perfection and Baltimore Grinding) recently started to do this. Perhaps it would make sense for you to contact them about their programs.
Research	Although your reputation for the highest-quality products in your industry continues, do you feel your reputation for service may have slipped? As a pseudo-consultant, I called on half-a-dozen major electrical equipment buyers and found very favorable comments about Marshall's [a competitor] new warehouse and computerized parts-control setup, as contrasted with long delays in parts availability that you and Dominion seem plagued with.
Ask for action	I am very interested in the possibility of joining Federal as Sales Manager. I feel that I am well qualified for the position. It sounds like a very challenging role, and I hope that we can meet again and explore the matter in greater depth.

I will call you on Friday the 15th, if I haven't heard from you, about our next meeting.

Sincerely,

161

If an inappropriate question is asked about your personal situation (child care, other family responsibilities such as an ailing parent, political opinions), defuse it by asking, "Is this a concern that relates to the position?" You may get some perspective on the interviewer's reason for asking such a question. Make any answer as noncontroversial as possible.

Try to avoid being interviewed on the phone before a face-to-face interview. Usually the interviewer is doing some preliminary screening to see if your experience and salary requirements are in the ballpark. Suggest that such questions can be better addressed in a personal interview. Usually it's hard to avoid such a phone interview when you're called.

Don't be surprised if you are asked to take a test, which may be a key part of the hiring process in some companies. Point out that you may be rusty on such tests, so your performance may be worse than it has been on the job. Here are some aids for taking tests:

- Don't panic, even though you're rusty. You'll probably do perfectly well.

- Make sure you understand the instructions and the rules. Don't be embarrassed to ask questions about what you are to do on the test, any time limit, and the scoring. For example, do they deduct incorrect answers from right answers or do they merely count correct answers?

- Make sure you plan your time properly on the tests. Sometimes people do poorly because they spend too much time on some parts and too little on others.

- Spend a minute or two looking over the whole test to decide how to distribute your time.

- Psychological tests are looking for personal characteristics, interests, or aptitudes. There's no right or wrong answer. Answer the questions honestly; one or two unfavorable answers probably won't make a lot of difference.

CHAPTER 13

CONDUCTING AN EFFECTIVE SEARCH

GETTING STARTED

The several weeks you've spent thoroughly preparing is now about to pay off. You've clarified your objective and priorities, written a strong resume, listed and prioritized your contacts, and prepared for interviews. Now is the time to apply your new skills and improve them.

Make your job search your top priority. Fit your personal activities (chores, doctor's appointments, and so on) around the disciplined campaign you must conduct.

Fill up your calendar as soon as you can—a minimum goal of seven appointments a week. You've seen how to improve your skills in getting interviews with people and in making a favorable impression on them.

In an early morning meeting, Tony Nagarro told me he had to leave at 9:30 because he had five more appointments that day. Three weeks later, Tony called to say that he had two excellent offers. Sustaining the number of appointments at a high level is a full-time job: It takes a lot of time to call (usually repeatedly) to set up appointments, to commute to and from them, participate in them, research the companies, send out thank-you notes, and critique each interview. But getting to see a lot of key people is doable and a key to completing a successful search in a reasonable time.

That this number of appointments can be achieved is confirmed by James E. Challenger, the CEO of a top outplacement firm, in his *The Challenger Guide—Job Hunting Success for Mid-Career Professionals*, (Contemporary Books, 1999). He urges 10 to 15 meetings with contacts and bona fide job interviews a week for midcareer professionals.

You'll find these interviews a great source of help in the advice you receive and in referrals to other useful sources of help and ultimately a job which will be a choice from several possibilities. Particularly useful sources are a good job support workshop, former and current job hunters, and perhaps a couple of executive recruiters. These meetings are in addition to those with your own contacts and people they introduce you to, key people you know and will meet. Many of these people are very knowledgeable on various aspects of a job search, and they will act as advisors and critics, be supportive, and will introduce you to others.

The key is that you have to take the initiative to get this help.

This chapter discusses a series of techniques that will help you conduct your search most effectively. These techniques will show you how to improve your use of time, how to make better decisions, how to improve your productivity, and how to become a more effective self-critic.

Working in a Different Environment

What's different? You're completely on your own. Before, you had an office with the sources of support and colleagues that were most necessary for you to succeed. You had a full day's work carrying out your responsibilities, attending meetings and responding to inquiries and requests made of you. Now none of this happens. Anything that happens occurs on your own initiative, including getting the support you need.

Job hunting in midcareer is more difficult than earlier in your career because companies do much less recruiting for employees at this stage. This has become more true in the last decade with the considerable layoffs of middle and senior management. The difficulty has increased because many of these management jobs have been eliminated. This means that not only are there many good people looking for jobs at these levels but also that there are fewer jobs available. When companies do recruit for these jobs, they have high hiring standards, and they are using very competitive screening techniques (executive recruiters, their own recruiters, and the Internet). These sources probably represent about 10 percent of the hiring for midcareer people. Test the waters with recruiters, answering ads and the Internet, but spend most of your time networking.

To be successful at it, you've got to contact a wide group of people, starting with people you know, then branching out to others they introduce you to. At the same time you should maintain a balance in your life. The only people you're answerable to are yourself, your family, and a very few friends who are particularly interested in trying to help.

You'll discover all kinds of temptations, now that your time is your own, like tackling home projects you've wanted to do for years. If you do a project, limit it. You've got a big job ahead of you. A week of vacation is OK, but it won't be as much fun as it is when you take time off before starting your new job. The longer you take off, the more rusty you'll get. You're going to need to be at your sharpest in your search.

What to Expect

One or two jobs may emerge early on, even promising ones. The reality of the job market is that these jobs usually soon fade away or turn out to be poor fits for you.

Start by contacting people you know quite well, who are receptive and who try to be helpful. A decade ago, many of these people may not have been through job searches themselves and had only a general understanding of the process. Today, a much larger number of them will have had this experience and will likely be empathetic and knowledgeable.

Expect considerable pressure and lots of ups and downs in your emotions—it's normal. Your best tonic is working hard and developing a full calendar. Expect several job prospects that seem close to an offer suddenly disappear. Less frequently, a prospect you thought was dead months ago comes to life again. Several months into your search, you may have gone through most of your contacts and their referrals, which are fewer and weaker than they were at the beginning. It's par for the course. Your advantage is that you've had more experience with this process now, have better skills, and are more resourceful in getting to see people you want to. Continue developing new contacts, but also go back to some of the more useful people you've already seen for additional help. Often you can contact a helpful person several times. That person will tell you if you are overdoing it.

You'll be running into indignities that you may have only occasionally run into before: rejection, people not answering or returning phone calls, indifference to your good record, and failure to follow through on promises. You'll also have to reveal personal things like your salary and some of the weaknesses in your record. Very likely you'll feel uncomfortable in certain social situations, yet they're important because they may offer opportunities for you. These experiences can make you feel indignant. Use this feeling to motivate yourself to make your job search a success. Turn an unpleasant feeling to your advantage: "I'm tired of being pushed around. I know I'm good. I've got the record to prove it." Become more assertive, creative, and astute in getting yourself across.

Don't expect people to keep promises. If some do, that's great, but many people won't, usually not maliciously but because once you've walked out of their office, they're deluged with higher priorities and feel they've already done their bit by seeing you. Be prepared for what looks like a promising lead that quickly disappears. Continue to fill up your schedule so that you always have one or two active possibilities and a number of appointments. This active agenda will keep your spirits up. If you don't maintain this momentum, a rejection from a promising lead can be a double loss: the loss of the job itself and the loss of your momentum. In general, don't waste time pursuing jobs that are unacceptable. Receiving any job offer, however, early on in your search, may boost your morale.

Several of the five to seven priorities that you originally identified may have changed. This is positive! It shows you've dug deeper in your thinking and have become more realistic. Revising of your priorities is important because it will help you make a better choice in the end.

Don't worry that being out of a job too long will affect your marketability. If you're conducting an active campaign and are seeing a lot of people, being out of work is just a part of corporate life these days.

When you've been turned down for a job, you may think it's because the employer feels your experience is too weak. In many cases, however, your experience is acceptable, but it's not exactly what they're looking for.

Beware of being side-tracked. Don't get carried away pursuing a possibility for months to the exclusion of everything else. It will be a real jolt if that possibility suddenly disappears. When one possibility becomes nearly all consuming, make a special effort to see other people and pursue other possibilities to keep your momentum up.

Several months into your search you may be tempted to take a temporary job or work as a part-time consultant. But meeting the demands of your temporary role and conducting a part-time search can be a difficult balancing act, so weigh the ramifications carefully. If such a situation looks like a realistic opportunity for permanent work, it would make more sense.

In general, work about 40 hours a week. If you're doing much less, you're hurting your chances. If you're doing more, you may burn out.

PERSONAL HABITS

Keep a daily diary to track appointments, followups, and expenses (for tax purposes). Organize your research notes on companies and your postinterview analyses so they're easy to find. If a lead you thought was dead gets revived with a phone call, you'll need the background information at your fingertips. Keep a careful record of each target contact with the name, address, phone numbers, and fax numbers. On each company record, track the date of each contact and your notes on it. Don't nickel and dime on expenses—particularly those that may result in a key step to a job.

Determine your most productive time of the day, and schedule your toughest activities at this time. For most people it's phoning for appointments. Obviously call for appointments when you're most likely to get through. The best times are likely to be before the start of the workday, at lunch time, or after the end of the regular workday, when you're less likely to be intercepted by a gatekeeper. Keep track of when you start your search activities each day, when you finish, and any long time off during the day, to ensure that you're really putting in the hours your job search demands.

Set realistic goals. You'll set yourself up for failure if you use the same standard in contacting people that you experienced when working. Use what you did last week as your standard. Reward yourself for good effort even though the results aren't as good as you'd like. Keep in mind some simple rewards: a walk, running a couple of errands, seeing a good friend, going to the mall, spending an hour on a hobby. Get regular exercise, even if only a walk—it's especially important with the pressure you're under. If you're really not putting in a good effort, penalize yourself by taking away some of your enjoyments for a while such as taking a walk or working on a pet project.

IMPROVING YOUR PRODUCTIVITY

Setting and Grading Daily Goals

Set goals that are a stretch, but doable.

Go public with them. You're much more likely to achieve your goals if you tell them to somebody. Get a friend to allow you to report your goals and your performance to him by e-mail—which the friend can treat as "junk mail." Grade your performance on each goal, on a scale from 1 to 10. When you get a poor grade (6 or below), do a "failure analysis" (page 171) on why it happened and identify ways to achieve a better result in the future. If you identify a specific reason for failing to meet goals frequently, add it to an improvement checklist on your daily goals list.

At the end of each day, set your goals for tomorrow. Make one of them your first activity and the time when you'll start it.

In setting your daily goals, ask yourself, "What are the one or two things that I'll be most upset about if I don't get them done today?"

Set a daily goal of two appointments, mostly networking meetings.

Set goals for the week. At the end of the week, review them in the same way.

Learn to use time between activities, brief segments of, say, a half-hour or an hour. Use this time from your fill-in activity list—a thank-you note, a phone call , and so on. This time is too valuable to waste.

Dialoguing

Dialoguing is a tool that helps you make better decisions by roughing out your thoughts in writing. There are three ways of dialoguing: a yes or no decision, a failure analysis, and a best-worst result.

EXHIBIT 13-1 • A Yes or No Decision Example

Should I contact Jack Avery of Optimum Floors (a promising lead that is long overdue)	
Yes	**No**
Jack could be useful.	But you've left 3 messages, and he hasn't responded.
I know, but he's busy. He may be away.	
	Maybe, but the last message was 3 days ago, so he's unlikely to call now unless I contact him again. I know, but why would he answer the fourth call when he hasn't answered the last three?
Maybe he won't but, I do know he won't answer the call if I don't even make it. I should call him. He could be useful.	
And it only takes a few minutes— I'm going to do it. I have little to lose.	

A Yes or No Decision. A yes or no decision is a way of deciding whether or not to take a certain action (see Exhibit 13-1). Start with a question about an action you're considering. Use dialoguing to explore the advantages and the disadvantages of your action. This process helps you make a decision by the yes side of your brain carrying on a dialogue with the no side. Write down the reason you have for wanting to take the action in the first place, an objection to that reason, a rebuttal to the objection, another objection, and so forth, until either yes or no wins the argument. Often a decision is very close, like 55 to 45. Act on it and move on.

Failure Analysis. A second way of using dialoguing to help make decisions is conducting a failure analysis, which is a technique to improve your plan for an activity (say, an interview) beforehand. In failure analysis, you analyze the possibility that the activity will be unsuccessful, identify the things that could go wrong, and prepare creative ways of dealing with each one. Because you'll be prepared for

EXHIBIT 13-2 • A Failure-Analysis Example

If I fail in my interview with Jane Teller of Acme and Teller Company, what are likely reasons and how could I have avoided that failure?	
Likely Reasons for Failure	**What Might I Wish I'd Done Differently**
I didn't know things I should have known about Teller.	Read Brown Brothers study of recent problems in industry. Talked to Jones, an acquaintance working for Superior Company (a competitor). Talked to Graves of Second National Bank.
I let Teller concentrate on me. I did not get her to reveal her concerns, that may represent an opportunity.	Prepared a list of questions to get Teller to talk of her company's problems.
I didn't find out Teller's reservations	Invited criticism (page 105). about me.
I don't know her next move.	Asked Teller what happens next.
You get rejected.	Used one of the strategies for turning around a rejection.

several kinds of failure, your chances for success improve. Failure analysis is useful for analyzing what you could have done better, say, in an interview after the fact, and what you'll try to avoid next time. Use it before every networking and job interview (see Exhibit 13-2).

To stimulate your thinking, ask yourself, "Is there any other possible reason for failure?" and "Are there any other ways of forestalling this failure?"

Failure analysis can also help in setting priorities.

A Best-Worst Decision. Doing a dialogue for evaluating a best-worst decision can also be useful. Ask yourself, "If I take this action I'm considering, what's the worst thing that could happen?" For example, "I had my first interview with Miracle Fabrics two weeks ago, and I haven't heard whether I made the next round. If I contact them, what's the worst thing that could happen?" Write out a dialogue of the best result versus the worst result to decide whether or not to take the action.

Overcoming Procrastination

One of the problems you face in a job search is putting off things that may be distasteful or frustrating. Here are three ways to reduce procrastination: multiple mentions, next steps, and decreasing time frames.

Multiple Mentions. In setting your daily goals, mention something more than once, to emphasize it, to put more pressure on yourself to do it, as shown in Exhibit 13-3. For example, if you have missed an important goal for several days, the next day write down that goal twice. If you miss it again the next day, write it down three times. Psychologically, you're more likely to tackle a goal that's mentioned three times than one that is mentioned once because by completing it,

EXHIBIT 13-3 • Multiple Mentions

Wed. 10/18

  Schedule
  10:00 Henry Taylor
  3:00   Martha Stiles

  Goals
  1. Prepare for Stiles interview
  2. Call Frank about Fairview
  3. Do research on Fairview

Thurs. 10/19

  Schedule
  9:30   Jack Ingersoll
  2:00   Merry Crosby

  Goals
  1. Do research on Fairview Software
  2. Do research on Fairview
  3. Do research on Fairview
  4. Set up appointments:
        Jones
        Carter
        Melton
  5. Thank-you letter:
        Ingersoll
        Crosby
        Danforth

---

you cross off three goals from your list. Notice that the October 19 goal, "Do research on Fairview" is repeated twice.

Next Step. To accomplish a task you've kept putting off, ask yourself, "What's the first step?" When you've completed it, ask "What's the next step?" Then when the second step is done, "What's the next step?" Doing this continually until it's done, you put teeth in accomplishing the series of steps by the third tool, "decreasing time frames."

Decreasing Time Frames. Put a time limit on the first step. If you run over the limit, put a short deadline on completing it. Then set a more realistic deadline on the second step and decreasing the next deadline, if you fail to meet it. By setting these deadlines, you'll be more focused on pushing what's needed to be done to accomplish it faster.

Using these tools can help improve your productivity considerably. Get familiar with them. Learn to use several that you've found helpful. It takes only a few minutes a day to use them, yet they'll help you make better decisions and stay more focused.

At the end of the week, spend 20 minutes reviewing the week's activities, recording them, and evaluating your progress or lack of progress:

+ Did you do better than you did the week before?
+ Did you meet all of your goals for this week? If not, why not?
+ What are your goals for next week?
+ Do have more irons in the fire than you did a week ago?
+ Are you getting in to see people more easily?
+ Are you getting better results with those that you do see?

Working at home presents problems for many people because there are just too many distractions; frequent reminders of things that need to be done, projects you've already put off for a long time, routine housework, television, books you've been meaning to read, and the comings and goings of family members.

GETTING HELP

Use your network to find a good job hunting workshop. Test several to find one with the kind of resources you want and a *positive atmosphere*. Usually they have a weekly meeting that can be instructive. Ask the head of the clinic for names of some of the successful graduates, particularly those in your field, and network with those people. Get to know other participants in the workshop who may know other people in your field, but stay away from participants with negative attitudes.

Develop a buddy system with a couple of impressive job hunters. Meet every two weeks for a cup of coffee and exchange ideas, names of people to contact, solutions to particular problems, and moral support.

Exec-U-Net is a quite comprehensive job support activity that offers a variety of services for a fee:

+ Job listings
+ Contact with thousands of executive recruiters
+ Frequent networking meetings in major metropolitan areas

For more information, contact execunet.com. You might find it useful to explore its services at one of their local workshops or through your network.

Get a list of useful Internet sources for jobs, company research, bulletin boards, and chat rooms. Some can be very useful, others a waste of time. Get advice from your network on the most helpful ones. Limit surfing, which can be a tremendous timewaster.

Engage a couple of trusted friends as advisors to meet with you once a month and take an occasional phone call. The people who would be most helpful are probably very busy, so don't wear out your welcome. They can provide you with good support, however, so use them regularly, but be sensitive of their time.

Be visible at your church, at community meetings, at your child's school activities, and so on. If anyone inquires about your search, ask if you can meet with him or her. But don't initiate this conversation. The same applies to social occasions.

Business meetings are different. Actively seek help. Have a calling card, and exchange it with others. Ask to meet with anyone appropriate.

Contact people again whom you saw four to six weeks earlier. Some will be responsive if you made a favorable impression and have kept them properly informed.

Use trade associations, particularly ones in your field, such as the Financial Executives Institute or the American Marketing Association. Even though you're not a member, if you know someone who is, you may be able to attend their meetings—a good source of contacts—as a guest.

CHECKLIST FOR A DRAGGING CAMPAIGN

Sometimes your campaign may be dragging. Once a month, use the checklist in Exhibit 13-4 to evaluate your campaign systematically.

EXHIBIT 13-4 • Checklist for Evaluating Your Campaign

Checklist	Ranking 1 to 10 Highest	Steps to Improve Grades 6 or Lower	Page Number
Search Preparation			
Are you clear on your priorities?		If not, review the priorities exercise.	25
Are you clear on what kind of job you're looking for?		If not, review alternative careers analysis.	23, 38
Are you getting negative comments on your resume?		If it has happened frequently, consider revising it.	81
Is your record keeping orderly?		Can you find the file if a company calls?	20
Use of Time			
Are you setting goals daily and grading them and the performance improvement checklist?		Develop and use them.	169
Are you starting your search first thing in the morning?		Don't waste the most productive time.	
Are you working 6–7 hours a day?		If you're not, start doing it.	168
Is your office set up to be efficient?		If not, reorganize it.	
Are you spending most of your working time outside the house?		If not, start doing it.	20
Are you setting goals and a time limit for the Internet?		If not, start doing it.	124
Sources of Help			
Have you found a good support workshop?		If you can't find one, see if you can locate a couple of buddies.	
Are you regularly asking networking contacts for useful people and organizations?		If not, review steps on how to get referrals.	102

EXHIBIT 13-4 • Checklist for Evaluating Your Campaign *(continued)*

Checklist	Ranking 1 to 10 Highest	Steps to Improve Grades 6 or Lower	Page Number
Sources of Help (continued)			
Have you got the continuing support of several trusted (knowledgeable) friends?		If not, select several to approach and ask them.	6
Are you regularly in touch with current and former job hunters?		If not, do it—they're often the most knowledgeable and supportive.	
Have you asked several what they found was most helpful in keeping a positive outlook?		If not, why not?	
Who are the 3 most helpful people you've found?		Identify them. Are you using them effectively?	
Have you been in touch with each within the month?		If not, why not?	
Getting Interviews			
Are you getting any interviews for actual jobs by contacting executive recruiters ?		Unless somewhat successful, concentrate on networking and blind prospecting.	
Are you getting any interviews sending letters in answer to ads?		Ditto.	
Are you getting any interviews answering Internet ads?		Ditto.	
Are you spending at least 75% of your time networking?		Keep a daily tally in your appointment book.	88
Are you having at least 7 job or networking interviews a week?		Keep a daily tally in your appointment book.	2
Are you averaging 2 referrals from every networking interview?		Keep a daily tally in your appointment book.	102

(continues)

EXHIBIT 13-4 • Checklist for Evaluating Your Campaign *(continued)*

Checklist	Ranking 1 to 10 Highest	Steps to Improve Grades 6 or Lower	Page Number
Getting Interviews *(continued)*			
Are you getting contacts to make the introduction of you to referrals?		If not, why not?	103
Are you getting to see more than 3/4 the people you approach in networking?		Have you discussed it with a helpful person?	
Have you contacted all the people you know who've conducted a job search in the last couple of years?		What percentage?	
Have you regularly asked network contacts for useful people and organizations for job hunters?		Do it when you see particularly useful people?	103
Have you identified the most productive way to get job interviews?		Think about it. Should you be directing your efforts differently?	
Are you getting Hiring Manager interviews from answering ads?		If you're not doing it, try it a few times. It can be very productive.	125
Have you reviewed the best sources of ads three months back?		If not, do it.	127
Have you gotten several interviews from every batch of 25 target letters?		Identify others who have, and discuss it with them.	113
Are you getting at least 2 job interviews a month?		Ditto.	
Are you converting refusals for face-to-face interviews into phone interviews?		If not, discuss it with someone who has done it successfully.	99

EXHIBIT 13-4 • Checklist for Evaluating Your Campaign *(continued)*

Checklist	Ranking 1 to 10 Highest	Steps to Improve Grades 6 or Lower	Page Number
Interview Preparation			
Do you review the interview preparation checklist, at the beginning of Chapter 12 before each job interview?		Do it.	149
Do you have a good understanding of a company's likely problems before an interview?		Research company on the Internet or with a broker.	142
Are you getting good information on interviewers before interviews?		Research through your workshop, your trade association, or a broker.	143
Conducting Interviews			
Are you using the invitation to criticism in networking?		If not, try it. Ask for advice from others on getting more candid criticism.	105
Have you developed good rapport with Hiring Manager's assistants?		Are you trying to engage them in chit-chat; have you sent each a thank-you letter?	156
Are you converting one-half of your job interviews into second interviews?		If not, have you discussed it with others who are doing it successfully?	
In job interviews, are you asking, "Where do we have a fit, and where don't we have a fit?"		Do it. Are you successfully dealing with their reservations?	154
Are you asking for the "next step" in job interviews?		If not, try it.	155
If you get rejected, are you making a good effort to stay in contention?		If not, review rejection alternatives.	156

(continues)

EXHIBIT 13-4 • Checklist for Evaluating Your Campaign *(continued)*

Checklist	Ranking 1 to 10 Highest	Steps to Improve Grades 6 or Lower	Page Number
Conducting Interviews (continued)			
Are you doing postinterview analysis?		You should every time!	157
Are you writing a prompt thank-you letter after each job and networking interview?		You should every time!	157
Are you writing an upon-further-reflection letter after every job interview?		You should every time!	157
Have you gotten feedback on any interviews from third parties?		If your interview reveals a mutual friend, ask him or her to inquire for you discreetly.	
Is how you're dressed and your physical appearance acceptable?		If not, correct it.	
Are any references hurting you?		If you have a doubt on any, ask a friend to conduct a blind reference check for you.	
Are you getting good responses to your PARs?		If key ones are falling flat, try describing them differently.	66
Are you using your universal skills in interviewing?		Are you identifying critical ones for the interviewer? Are you using a PAR to overcome the interviewer's concern?	146
Are you getting interviewers to bring up their problems in your field of expertise?		Ask several leading questions to get them to reveal their concerns.	101, 109

EXHIBIT 13-4 • Checklist for Evaluating Your Campaign *(continued)*

Checklist	Ranking 1 to 10 Highest	Steps to Improve Grades 6 or Lower	Page Number
Conducting Interviews *(continued)*			
Have you conducted mock interviews with friends or volunteer counselors?		If not, try it. Ask, "What are your 2 or 3 top priorities in a candidate" —say, in meeting dead-lines, or overcoming difficulties in getting a job done.	148
Are you identifying the interviewer's biases?		If not, why not? Work on it.	152
Is the interviewer doing most of the talking in interviews?		If not, why not? Work on it.	
Are you defusing likely hidden issues—such as age, lack of specific experience?		Are you trying to defuse them? If not, do it.	153
How well are you selling yourself?		Do you feel most interviewers are reacting favorably to you? If not, try a different approach?	
Are you critiquing each interview?		Do it. Ask yourself what you could have done better.	108
Miscellaneous			
Are you regularly discussing progress with your spouse or partner?		If not, at least once a month do it. Try to address any concerns.	
Are you keeping your references informed?		Are you talking with each every 6 weeks or so to keep them in the loop?	
Are you getting regular exercise and diversion?		You should be. You're working long hours under a lot of pressure. You need some change.	
Are you limiting your eating and drinking?		This could really set you back. Be very careful about it.	

CHAPTER 14

EVALUATING OFFERS AND MAKING THE FINAL DECISION

THE PROCESS

You're at a point at which your search over the last months will become a success or a failure. You've got an offer, hopefully more than one so you can make a choice. Having a choice considerably reduces the chance of making a mistake.

One underemphasized aspect of a job search is that a high percentage of new jobs last a short time, often less than a year. Several years ago, in a little over a year, I had 11 candidates whose prior job had lasted less than a year. They were all middle- or senior-level managers with an MBA or law degree from a well-known university, and none of them had had a major job problem before. Three of them had taken jobs that required relocating: pulling their children out of their schools, selling their houses, and moving to another part of the country. These job hunters were not shortsighted, unsophisticated people, and yet their new jobs failed.

When these 11 people told me of their experiences, I asked them each two questions. First, "When did you realize that you had made a poor choice?" Several of them said within the first week, and most of the others said within the first month. Second, "Looking back on this experience, were there warning signs?" Most of them said, in retrospect, there were, but they had underestimated them. Sometimes they recognized the problems, but they thought they could deal with them.

An associate counseled a CEO from a badly depressed area to accept another CEO position across the country. This man had visited the company twice for several days each time and had intensive talks with the two owners and other key people. At the end of his first day on the job, however, he resigned. The job had been misrepresented. He had been told he would have full control of the whole operation, but he immediately realized that the two "absentee" owners intended to run the show. Also they already exposed him to several unethical dealings of theirs that he couldn't live with.

These experiences demonstrate a problem all job hunters face: the difficulty of knowing what's really going on in a company they are considering joining. Finding and accepting a new job involves a courtship on both sides: The candidate tries to make the most favorable impression possible, and the company often romances the candidate until the offer is accepted.

Your best insurance against the disasters that befell these executives is to get as much information as you can to evaluate the company and your prospective boss thoroughly and confirm that the job meets most of your priorities.

The success of all your hard work to date may depend on how successfully you carry out the steps described in this chapter.

STALLING OFFERS

Negotiate for as long a period as possible before you have to answer an offer. Get at least two weeks; a month is better. Many companies aren't giving as much time today as they have in the past. Actually it's to your and the company's advantage that you be given a reasonable time, so that when you say yes, you're comfortable with the decision. If a company gives you an unreasonably limited time to answer them, you may question how attractive the company would be to work for.

Between an offer and your acceptance, you have a good opportunity to get more information on the company, possibly improve the offer, and get another for comparison. Get your due, but don't overdo it.

GETTING MORE INFORMATION ON THE JOB AND COMPANY

Between getting the offer and accepting it, improve your understanding of the company, the boss, and the job. Discuss these issues with a couple of insiders and a couple of outsiders. Find one or two insiders (current or former employees) you may know or can get introduced to and discuss the company with them delicately, as it could be awkward if word got back to the company. Ask them about the history of the job, the problems as they see them, and information on your prospective boss, whose personality is important because of the close association you'll have if you take this job. Find out as much as you can. What's the boss's style? Demanding? A stickler for detail? Ask the question, "What's the boss like?" to several who know her. People when asked this question don't like to be critical. First you're likely to get a bland answer. "She's OK and very competent." To get the most realistic answer, use the Rule of Four. By repeating the same question three times, slightly varying the wording, you may finally get, "She's really tough. Nobody is happy working for her"—the information you sought.

Also talk to outsiders, people who are likely to have a general knowledge of the company, such as bankers, lawyers, stockbrokers, suppliers, trade association members, and job hunters. Ask about the company's general reputation, its performance, and its future prospects. Be sure you're comfortable with the industry and with the company's position in it. Is it firmly established, improving its position in the industry, or at least holding its own?

If you still have reservations about the company or the job, discuss them with a trusted friend and a friendly recruiter or both. Ask these people and one or two active trade association members whether the compensation package is reasonable (see "Negotiating Compensation" later in the chapter).

USING AN OFFER TO GET OTHERS

Conduct a sweep of the possible jobs you think you're in contention for. This sweep is particularly important if the offer you have in hand isn't as good as you feel you deserve or you have other major reservations about it. If you're unlikely to accept the offer in hand, this approach is risky because you may jeopardize several potential jobs you're a candidate for. If you've got an acceptable offer but think you can get a better one, a sweep is worth doing. Because of your limited time, you have to move very fast. Try the possibilities you've been working on.

You may have a pretty good offer from Company A, one you probably would accept, but one that's not what you had hoped for. Meanwhile, you think Company B may be close to making you a better offer. You have nothing to lose in telling Company B you'd prefer to work for them but you have an acceptable offer that you have to answer by such and such a date. Ask Company B, if it's really interested in you, can it speed up the process?

For example, Richard Murray had a fair offer from Docking Corp., one that he was planning to accept but had reservations about. He also had to give them an answer in two weeks. Also Richard had been interviewed several times by Angell Company to be its Executive VP and was told that they were interested in him but that an offer would take time because the Chairman, CEO, and two outside directors had to agree on the choice. He called his contact at Angell and said he had an acceptable offer from another company though he preferred Angell and that he had to respond to it in 10 days. Two days later, Richard had the offer he wanted from Angell. If Company B has a substantial interest in you, it may be able to move up its timetable. It's a mistake not to ask.

Sometimes the company you're in the process of leaving makes a counteroffer to keep you. Evaluate it, like any other offer, against your priorities. Occasionally, your company makes a counteroffer just to stall until they get your replacement. However, sometimes, an almost-former employee stays, and it turns out to be a long-term happy relationship.

NEGOTIATING COMPENSATION

When you get an offer, consider whether or not to try to upgrade it. Most companies are used to this negotiation, but occasionally a company gets upset and withdraws the offer.

Negotiating with a future employer on compensation can put you in a delicate position. In buying a house or a car, your involvement with the seller is only on that particular transaction. In the case of a job, however, you are negotiating with those who you're going to work closely with if you accept the offer.

After you've made your sweep of possibilities and have gotten better insight into the company, you may want to request a meeting with the Hiring Manager to improve the offer. The HM may think you have a lot of things you want to negotiate, so right off, you should name the few key items you want to discuss to put him at ease and increase the chance that each item will get serious consideration.

To make the best impression, express genuine enthusiasm about the company, its people, and the job. If you do that, it may help somewhat to get the best concessions. Before you get into salary negotiations you should determine the minimum that's acceptable. Never ask for a salary lower than what you had before. Try to learn the salary range for the position.

Salary

At this stage you already have the salary offer, and the interviewer knows your prior compensation. You want to handle any salary negotiations carefully. You can get the offer increased, but if you push too hard, it often can come back to haunt you. A salary concession that is too large is the most likely issue your boss may hold against you in the future.

During the discussion you might want to say, "One of the reasons I left XYZ was that I felt I was making outstanding contributions, but I got the same percentage raise as several people who were just doing average jobs. I want to work for a company where contributions are fairly rewarded. Are merit increases here really for merit, or does everybody get the same percentage?" This may make the boss think more carefully about your future increases if you're doing a really good job.

Often you're better off to accept a small increase and say, "That's a disappointment. But it's acceptable if my salary can be reviewed in six months." Then try to get a concession in getting your vacation increased from two to three weeks or another fringe benefit that's important to you.

Fringe Benefits

Fringe benefits are an important part of negotiations. Sometimes it's easier to get concessions on them than on the salary itself. Some of the possibilities are the following:

- A salary review in six months rather than a year
- Your decision-making authority
- The support and budget you'll get
- Your reporting relationship
- Your title
- Bonuses and stock options
- A hiring bonus

Beware of uncertain items such as bonuses and options unless the company has been doing well and has good prospects. In recent years, these enticements have often proved worthless.

Relocation Expenses

Moving expenses are substantial. Who pays for them is negotiable. Well-financed companies tend to be reasonably generous, and the larger the company, the more standardized the policy is likely to be. Moving expenses include travel and lodging costs for house-hunting trips, moving costs, temporary housing costs, a potential loss on selling your house, purchasing a new home (especially if you're moving to a location with substantially higher housing costs), an allowance for getting settled, a higher cost-of-living subsidy, a bridge loan if your house doesn't sell, and outplacement and job assistance for a spouse. Have a reasonable and documented estimate of these expenses when you negotiate them. Large companies requiring key people to move frequently are much more knowledgeable about these issues than smaller companies.

Severance Packages

Although negotiating a severance package before you start a new job is awkward, companies often include severance in the compensation package for key people, especially if you're being hired away from an important job at a stable company. Severance is particularly important if you're relocating for this job.

Figure out how much money you would need at your present standard of living for at least six months.

Employment Contracts

Such agreements are quite common for higher-level jobs. With these complex issues, consider engaging an employment legal specialist.

Noncompete Provisions

Be careful that you don't hurt your future marketability.

EVALUATING OFFERS

Ideally, you'll have at least two offers to compare with each other. Frequently, though, you'll have one offer and a better one pending. In evaluating offers, include the potential one.

Exhibit 14-1 (pages 192–193) shows the decision Tom Franks was faced with. Start this evaluation by updating your priorities. Grade each company on each priority. Add up the total score for each company, and compare it with your gut feeling. If ABC's offer feels better than Monarch's offer, yet Monarch's score is higher, reexamine the percentage of importance you've given to each priority and the scores you've given each company on each priority. Make sure the numbers represent your true feelings by reconciling the scores with your gut feelings. It's particularly important to run this analysis by one or two trusted friends. After you're comfortable with your job analysis, if Monarch seems to be the best, as it does in Exhibit 14-1, "Alternative Jobs Analysis," make a determined effort to land that position.

If you've done a good job of evaluating these three offers, you'll see why salary isn't necessarily the deciding factor.

Sometimes you have a mediocre offer only after a long search and have to decide whether to accept it. Your decision depends on a number of factors, such as how long you've been looking, how well your job search has been going lately, your family and financial situation, and what other prospects you have. If you accept a mediocre offer, you may have that job for a long time and may start a future search with downgraded marketability.

In general, accept a job offer only if you're pretty comfortable with it.

AFTER THE FINAL DECISION

In accepting an offer, ask for it to be put in writing. Most employers feel it's a reasonable request.

After you've accepted the offer, phone or write a thank-you letter to your network, contacts, and references, but be careful on its timing. If your decision to take this job was shaky, hold off thanking people for a few weeks. In case you leave this job in a short time, as occasionally happens, you may want to be able to act as though your job search is continuing without interruption. Obviously, after you accept one offer, you have to turn down the others. If your final decision was difficult, turn down the other offers in a way that gives you the best chance of retrieving the offer later if necessary. Explain to each company that your rejecting it was a very, very hard decision because you were impressed with the company and the job offer, but you finally decided to accept this other offer for personal or logistical reasons, such as not having to move or requiring too much or not enough travel.

Mary Parson had five offers when she left the prestigious national consulting firm she was working for. Her Alternative Jobs Analysis eliminated two immediately, and another shortly thereafter. She chose Parnell Company, which had recently gone through several years of turmoil but had a new CEO with an optimistic plan. The other final candidate was Newman Cox, a Fortune 500 company with an excellent long-term record. After three months, Mary was fired by Parnell. Here's where Mary's tactful handling of her turndown of Newman Cox's offer paid off. With a careful plan, Mary approached Newman Cox again and was delighted when, after several weeks, she was offered the same job and compensation that she had previously turned down. Five years later, she's still there, is happy, and has been given a major promotion.

What has been covered to date has been based on the assumption that you're conducting an active campaign, usually because you've been let go. The next chapter discusses a situation in which you're unhappy and you are thinking of leaving your current employer.

EXHIBIT 14-1 • Alternative Jobs Analysis for Tom Franks

Your Priorities	Rating	My goal	Production Manager, ABC Metals	
Status		Actual offer		Actual offer; answer by 3/15
The job (responsibilities)	18	Planning—not line	14	Work I enjoy and do well; lower level than I'd like
Company's status and future prospects	16	A well-established company in a strongly growing field	11	Fair; has had somewhat erratic record; but with some growth; in a very competitive field
Starting salary and fringe benefits	14	$95,000–$105,000	9	$98,000 + 5% to 10% bonus
Company's reputation as a place to work	12	Known as fair people; low turnover and few layoffs	7	Poor; has had quite high turnover; has reputation as being tough people to work for
Type of boss and close associates	11	Prefer high-grade professionals who are open and direct	6	Didn't like 2 of the 5 people I met; liked prospective boss; not really my kind of people
Location	9	Don't want to move	7	No immediate move; possibly later
Base to move from (if job fails)	7	Broadly needed skills; well-respected co.	5	Broadly needed skills in company with mediocre reputation
Personal demands of job (pressure, time, demands, traveling)	6	Medium pressure, less than 10% traveling; mod. overtime acceptable	3	Lots of pressure and overtime; little traveling
Future salary and fringe benefits	4	Good long-term prospects	3	Moderate risk; good salary-increase prospects
Opportunity for promotion	3	Reasonable prospects for promotion	2	Good chance to become Superintendent in 4 years
Total	100			67

Numerical Value and Description	
Facilities Planning Manager, Monarch Co.	**Plant Superintendent, Foremost Machine**
Offer seems close	Actual offer; answer by 3/18
16 Work I enjoy and do well; staff work like this is my strength; report to senior person	10 Work I like less; is less suited to my interests and strengths; acceptable level in organization
14 Excellent; is known as a very well run company; consistent growth, preeminent in a strong industry	7 Poor; company has had weak record in last several years; seems way behind times
7 $95,000 + 7% bonus	10 $100,000 + 5% to 10% bonus estimated
12 Very good; low turnover; no real layoffs, known as good place to work	11 Good; moderate layoffs and turnover; used to have much better reputation than now
10 Liked all the people I met; was very favorably impressed by my prospective boss; they're my kind of people	8 Liked everyone, though several of them didn't seem very professional; quite a bit of nepotism
9 No immediate move nor likely in long run	9 No immediate move nor likely in long run
4 Very specialized skills in company with excellent reputation	5 Broadly needed skills in company with fair reputation
3 Medium pressure and overtime; 20% travel	3 Medium pressure and overtime; no traveling
2 Low risk; moderate but steady salary increases	2 High risk; good salary-increase prospects
1 Very little chance, but steady growth will increase responsibility of job	1 Good chance to be Manufacturing Vice President in 7 years
78	66

CHAPTER 15

SHOULD YOU MAKE A JOB CHANGE? (If You Have a Choice)

So far this book has been based on the assumption that you're un-employed—or expect to be shortly—and are faced with getting a new job. Suppose, however, that you have a job, a secure one, but you aren't happy with it. We're now going to look into how you should go about dealing with this question. What do you do? There's usually a lot of risk and hard work in getting another job. The risk is even greater if you're employed because you'll give up some impor-tant things: your salary, security, and pleasant associations among other things.

Taking a job that will fall through in a short time, which is what happened to 11 of my clients, as already described, happens too fre-quently. Also, having a job complicates your job search because it limits the kind of search you can conduct.

A good adage is, "The devil you know is better than the devil you don't know." It isn't always true, but it's a good point of view to start with in contemplating leaving your company by choice. This chap-ter will show you how to methodically assess your situation. It will then advise you on some things you can do that, if done deliberately over a period of time, will make you a more effective employee and may improve your current job. At the very least, these steps should make you a more effective employee so you should be a more attractive candidate in a job search.

MYTHS ABOUT CHANGING JOBS

There are a number of misconceptions about changing jobs. Let's examine a few of them:

- *If you've had a strong, clean record in a company, you can expect that your good record will continue in a new job.* That probably will happen, but don't count on it.

- *If you've been unsuccessful in one company, you're better off taking a job with another company.* Not necessarily. Often similar problems at the first company reappear in the second company.

- *You're an exception, and you'll end up with a better job.* There's no guarantee.

- *You feel underpaid, and you're likely to earn more at another job.* Actually, the chances are probably against it. You'll also find your benefits aren't as good since some benefits like vacation are based on length of service.

- *You're unhappy in your current job, and you'll likely be happier in a new job.* Maybe, but in a year or two, you may well find that your situation hasn't improved that much.

- *You feel underutilized.* That may be so, but maybe you feel you're in that position now because you aren't stretching yourself to be useful enough to be singled out for better assignments.

- *Several companies have pursued you actively in the past, so you'll get a good job now.* Having being sought after is a plus, but has it happened recently? The fact that you stayed in your current job means that previous interest wasn't strong enough for you to make a change. Furthermore, you're older now and less likely to be pursued.

♦ *Time marches on. If I don't move pretty soon, it will be much more difficult later on.* Waiting may not make much difference, and your current job might improve in a year. You owe it to yourself to consider conducting an intense self-improvement program. If you take a year to spruce up your record, you'll be a more attractive candidate.

Some spot surveys made of attendees at job hunting workshops for Harvard Business School alumni revealed that roughly half of the attendees currently had jobs. When surveyed at the end of the workshop, most said they were less inclined to make a change than they were at the start of the workshop. Rather than starting a job search prematurely, work with a counselor (often an HR friend who'll moonlight) who can help you sort out your options and try to make your current job into what you're looking for. Several frank conversations with trusted friends could also be useful. You have little to lose working to improve your current situation and talking with trusted friends.

Perhaps you've just run out of gas on your current job and have let your performance fall off. Perhaps your unhappiness on your current job results from some other problem in your life.

If your job situation is going downhill, do something about it before you get into real trouble.

WHY ARE YOU FRUSTRATED?

You want to change jobs because you're unhappy about something. First, figure out what that something is, specifically. Don't just change the most obvious thing and expect that that it will cure your unhappiness. Before you go to the trouble of changing jobs, make sure it isn't yourself that needs changing.

197

To gain persective, do the self-assessment exercises in Chapter 3, "Determining Your Job Goals." Although these were presented in the context of a job search, they also apply to deciding whether you should make a job change. Pay particular attention to who you are, your likes and dislikes, your job requirements, and their priority and reasoning behind those priorities. Being guided by these priorities is the first step in getting a job that satisfies your fundamental interests and needs.

Identifying the reasons for your frustrations is important at this point. Paying attention to the key areas is necessary to develop a correction plan. You should identify what's upsetting you by rating your feelings on the common frustrations listed in Exhibit 15-1, "Common Reasons for Unhappiness on the Job."

The factors that you marked as major are what's bugging you. There may be no easy way to improve them without leaving the company. Even then, relief may be only temporary as they may be replaced by more difficult factors in a job search and then getting settled in on a new job.

YOUR IMPROVEMENT PROGRAM

If you stay on, it's unlikely you'll achieve your goals in the company unless you improve your performance considerably. Some people compensate for underachievement at work by getting personal satisfaction from hobbies or community activities. These activities may satisfy you, but they are unlikely to improve your job situation.

Consider improving your job performance, which will enhance your chances in the company, make you a more attractive candidate to other employers, and may renew your enthusiasm for your job.

Gain the support and recognition of the powerful people in the company who affect your job. Take a clinical and hard-nosed look at how you're dealing with the company's political situation.

Improve your ability to play politics effectively, to deal with the personalities and motivations of the people who are important to

Exhibit 15-1 • Common Reasons for Unhappiness on the Job

	Major Factor	Minor Factor	No Factor at All
1. You have gotten poor performance reviews.			
2. You have a personality conflict with your boss.			
3. Your job is not well suited to your. particular interests			
4. You get minimum merit raises, if any.			
5. You're not being challenged.			
6. You failed to get a promotion.			
7. You feel that you can earn more money elsewhere.			
8. Your division's activity is diminishing.			
9. You have personality conflicts with coworkers.			
10. There's no opportunity for further learning.			
11. There's no opportunity for professional development.			
12. The company is doing poorly.			
13. The company has downsized within the past year.			
14. Your job responsibilities haven't changed for 2 years.			
15. Other			

your success. Don't engage in backbiting, although some people have advanced themselves this way. Usually the people who are most critical of company politics are the people who don't play politics well.

Harry Felton was a successful politician in his company, but he would say his success had nothing to do with company politics. He would say that he disliked them and didn't consider himself effective in dealing with them. Nevertheless, he was universally respected for his ability and willingness to assist the many who sought his help.

Harry's success as a politician in the very best sense of the word was key to his high standing in the company.

Emulating someone like Harry Felton can improve your overall performance. Many people damage their performance by doing their work without being smart on how they handle themselves politically. Being able to read the politics of the organization and learning how to operate effectively in it is an important skill.

Being aware of who holds the power is important. Some power evolves from the formal organization (an individual's position on the organization chart) and some from the informal organization (the actual relationships that exist within the company). Observe the roles people play, who are continually asked for advice and are given special assignments, who has the power in various committees, who eats lunch with whom, and who socializes together in outside activities. The informal organization results from key individuals, the information pipeline, seniority, and personality as well as these personal relationships.

As an outsider, it's nearly impossible to assess the political environment in a new company. About the only thing that you may be able to learn during your interviews is whether the company is highly political. During the interview, most companies try to play their politics down.

After you've identified the power holders and learned what kind of people they are, ask yourself, "How strongly do you have their support?" If it isn't strong, can you change enough to win their support?

A key to your success is how your boss, call him Fred Sherman, feels about you. Let's look at your relationship with Fred, as well as the surrounding hierarchy (his boss, his influential peers, and so on). The key to Fred's feelings about you are how well you help him do what he has to do and wants to do. What does Fred's boss expect of him? What are Fred's goals? What are his priorities, the pressures on him, his relationship with other executives, his goals, and his biases? Understanding his needs is important to developing a positive relationship with him.

Write out answers to these questions. Whether or not you agree with his feelings and priorities, they're real and you have to deal with them.

How would Fred rate your performance? Work through the evaluation in Exhibit 15-2. For every item on which you get 6 or lower, write down why. Dialogue: If Fred left, would you get his job? If not, why not? You'll get a pretty good idea of how he sees you by your rating on these items.

Develop the discipline of setting daily goals. You've been shown the failure-analysis tool (Exhibit 13-2, p.171, on dialoguing), which can be helpful in goal setting. When you're planning your goals at the end of each day, ask, "If I fail to do tomorrow what I should do, what would be the likely reasons, and what would I wish I'd done differently?"

Daily grade your performance on how well you met each goal, say, on a scale of 1 to 10, 10 being highest.

As part of your exercise of setting your daily goals, include a section called "Your Personal Improvement Checklist" where you write the three or four items you most need to improve on. For every item with a grade of 6 or lower, visualize a personal consultant looking over your shoulder and saying, "Why did you give yourself a grade of 4 on *meeting deadlines?*" Also, "What are you going to do differently tomorrow?"

Daily when you're setting your goals for the next day, also grade your performance on your improvement checklist.

You'll soon be able to set up tomorrow's goals, grade today's performance, and dialogue about any low grades in 10 minutes. When you've made enough progress on each improvement item, you can remove it. This activity is well suited to your computer. *Excel* graphics provides a means for tracking your progress over a period of time.

EXHIBIT 15-2 • Rating Your Performance versus That of Your Peers

Rate your performance the way your boss would rate you, not the way you feel you should be rated.

1 Is Highest, to 5 Is lowest	1	2	3	4	5
What is your overall job performance?	___	___	___	___	___
How well do you do what the boss wants?	___	___	___	___	___
How well do you help him achieve his personal goals?	___	___	___	___	___
How sensitive are you to his biases?	___	___	___	___	___
How effectively do you communicate with him?	___	___	___	___	___
How proud is he to have you on his team?	___	___	___	___	___
How much of a real difference do you make?	___	___	___	___	___
How well do you set priorities and work toward them?	___	___	___	___	___
Do you only put out fires or do you anticipate problems?	___	___	___	___	___
How productive are you?	___	___	___	___	___
How often do you get bogged down with detail?	___	___	___	___	___
How good is your work?	___	___	___	___	___
How well motivated are you?	___	___	___	___	___
How often do you meet deadlines?	___	___	___	___	___
How effectively do you participate in meetings?	___	___	___	___	___
How effective are you in developing people?	___	___	___	___	___
How effective are you as a team player?	___	___	___	___	___
How easy are you to work for?	___	___	___	___	___
How much are you doing to broaden your vision?	___	___	___	___	___

Using your goals and checklist and dialoguing about your low grades will over time show you how to improve your performance. Don't expect miracles. But don't give up on the program. In several months you should see some real progress!

A key to improving your image is to improve your use of time. *BusinessWeek* recently stated, "Studies have shown that many people spend 80% of their time on the least important 20% of their jobs—and only 20% on work that is the 80% most important." Develop the discipline to spend as much time as you can on the most important tasks.

For three days keep track of your time in 15-minute increments. How much of your time went into things you have no control over? Be sure you ask yourself, "Did I really have no control over them?" "Did I spend more time than I needed on them?" "Why?" "What am I going to do differently in the future?" Are you spending too much time on projects you choose because they're easy to do so you can cross them off your to-do list? Be careful to avoid spending time on busy work rather than on the most important tasks.

Your goal is to free up more discretionary time to use on things that could have the biggest payoff for you. On any job, there's maintenance work, the things that are necessary to keep your job going, such as meeting with your staff, supervising them, and corresponding. The key is identifying time you could have used more effectively. Beware of allowing your subordinates to delegate upward, that is, dumping things on you they should do themselves.

Superstars are one or two people whose performance you particularly admire from your past or current experience. Visualize facing a tough problem or a situation in which you performed poorly and imagine how they would have dealt with it. Typically work falls into a pattern, developed over many years. This pattern isn't easy to break. Identify someone who impresses you with how much he gets done, say, Jack Seymour. Visualize Jack being on your job. How would he work to carry out your tasks, well but quicker. What can you learn from him? Changing your work habits is not a picnic, but using the goals and improvement checklist with hard-nosed discipline can increase your effectiveness—all to the benefit of your current situation.

Take a couple of minutes in the middle of the day to see how you're progressing on the day's goals and revise your afternoon accordingly.

Review the section "Improving Your Productivity" (pages 169 through 173) for ways to improve your performance. Here are a couple of other useful tools specifically applicable to on-the-job performance improvement. *Showcase* projects have the potential of getting you kudos that you usually don't get. These are projects that need to be done that aren't being worked on that can draw favorable attention to you. Test the general idea of each project with your boss to make sure it has showcase potential.

Make the most desirable *showcase* project the first priority for your discretionary time. List it as part of your daily goal. Pick things that will make your boss look good. It's important to get the credit for them by carrying them out well and communicating them discreetly to those individuals who most likely will influence your future.

Another area for improvement is your conduct in meetings. A considerable portion of your business life is probably spent in meetings: some regular committee meetings and other informal ones on projects. You should make valuable contributions in these meetings, particularly when your boss is present. Take advantage of these opportunities to shine.

To improve your meeting performance, first assess your current meeting performance. Do you contribute to thinking that's accepted and acted on? Are you properly prepared? Do you take controversial stands that antagonize the most powerful committee members? Do you come out of meetings kicking yourself for not having contributed to something in the discussion or not having initiated an important idea?

Analyze your meeting strengths and weaknesses and identify what you need to do to improve. Develop a meeting preparation checklist that also includes a section for grading your performance. Before important meetings, think of the likely agenda and prepare yourself to be knowledgeable about the items on it. Think of what you could contribute. Review the checklist and prepare for things that you can expect. Develop several questions or key points before a meeting to introduce at the appropriate time. Have them available in notes you take to the meeting. If you're expected to report, be prepared to deal with objections and possible questions. After each meeting, analyze what went on and evaluate your performance. How did you rate overall? Were there items you weren't prepared for? Why? Ask yourself, knowing what you know now, what do you wish you had done differently? What will you do differently next time? If you did not participate actively in the meeting, why not?

Finally, work on ways to improve your motivation. You may be too complacent or nonconformist. Visualizing the following scenario may jar you out of this complacency.

It's 4 o'clock on Friday afternoon, and the phone rings. It's your boss's assistant, who says Fred wants to see you. After a few pleasantries, Fred says, "Bill, I'm afraid I've got some bad news for you. You know we've been undergoing quite a change here at XYZ. I told you several times in the last year or so that your performance hasn't been what it should be. You've been here a long time and made quite a few contributions to the company over the years, but things change. Frankly, there's no longer a place for you in the company. I'm sorry to tell you this because we've known each other a long time, but you're being let go as of today. This decision is final. I've discussed this several times with Ralph Nolan (the CEO), and he agrees. I'm sorry it's come to this, but it may be the best thing for you in the long run."

If your motivation has been slipping, think of that scenario. It may be closer to reality than you think.

Another key part of your being is your personal life. Think about it also. Have you gotten into a rut? Are you getting enough satisfaction from your home life, social life, and hobbies? If not, the rest of your life can adversely affect your job performance. Try to improve the rest of your life so it will help your job performance. Expand your outside interests. Become active in the community, or take up a new hobby. Midcareer is a time when many expand their outside activities. Perhaps you should get involved in one or two. Just don't overdo it. Also, make increasing outside activities only one part of the improvement plan.

Don't expect this self-improvement program to realize great results overnight. It's going to take a lot of work. If you work hard for six months or a year, your self-improvement program *can* improve your job performance and job satisfaction and may make your current job into what you'd hope to find elsewhere. It will also improve your life overall.

You have nothing to lose in this self-improvement program and a lot to gain. In addition, the results and new skills will make you a more attractive candidate if you decide to change jobs. You may want to use a counselor who can help you get quicker and better results with such an improvement program.

GET ANOTHER JOB IN THE COMPANY

A lateral move within the same company can have lots of advantages. One of the best-known outplacement firms has found that about 10 percent of its clients end up accepting jobs with the company that recently fired them. In almost half the cases, the individuals have ended up with more responsible jobs and higher salaries. The outplacement program was a big factor in identifying these clients' skills and goals and improving their ability to sell themselves.

If you decide to seek another job, start by asking yourself the question, "Is there another job within the company that would satisfy my needs?" In most instances, there isn't, but sometimes there is. Start off by updating the self-assessment exercises in Chapter 3, "Determining Your Job Goals." If you've identified a particular area in your company that you think might be a better fit, talk to a key person in that function whom you're on good terms with. Prepare for this meeting as you would for a job interview. Explain your interest and your thoughts as to why you could be effective in the other functional area. Here again, be patient, but an offer might come in time.

If you want to change your functional area, say, from operations to finance, your best chance is to move within your company rather than changing to a new company.

HOW TO LEAVE YOUR COMPANY

If you decide to seek a job outside the company, decide whether to resign now or wait until you've found the other job. If you wait, you don't have much to lose. Getting a job with another company probably won't be easy, so start looking while you're still working. You're more attractive to prospective employers if you're still working. Executive recruiters used to shy away from job hunters who were out of work, but they are less likely to now because of the job turmoil of the last decade.

A problem in conducting a search while on the job is that you have to do it on the sly. You have only a limited amount of time to carry on your search, so you get less exposure and you may have little success. Don't underestimate the amount of preparation you'll need for a good search. Follow the steps in Chapters 2 through 6 to be effectively prepared. You must have a clear view of what you're looking for, develop a top-flight resume, and have a good plan.

Once you're well prepared, start your campaign with a limited number of contacts (your closest friends in influential positions, plus a few selected recruiters). Ask several of those friends for their suggestions, and ask that they be candid critics and if they'll allow you to meet with them several times. When you make your first contact, your job is at risk. You just won't know what the relationships each of your contacts might have with your boss or other people in your company. Expect your search to get discovered within one to three months of your seeing people outside. Therefore, select your contacts carefully, emphasize that your search is confidential, and be patient; job searches often take six months and can take years or more.

Prepare yourself for the possibility that your boss will discover you're looking. If your search is discovered, it may just be awkward, but be prepared for the worst: getting fired. The company's reaction depends on the company, the type of boss you have, and your relationship with him or her. You may be asked to leave immediately. You may be given a limited time to search and a deadline when you have to leave. You may even be encouraged to stay. Have a strategy if your boss calls you into his office and says, "I've heard you're looking for another job. What's going on?" There's no easy way to deal with this situation, but you might say, "I was approached on a possibility, and I did casually check it out. I decided that my situation here is much better, so I turned it down and intend to stay." You could also say, "For my long-term career plan, I feel I should casually check out the market every few years because it's hard to get perspective on my progress otherwise."

Be careful about choosing to leave during an economic recession. Obviously, the job market will be in turmoil and fewer companies will be hiring. During a recession, put your energy into improving your performance on the job so that when the market improves, you'll have better credentials for making a desirable change.

When you walk out the door for the last time, leave the most favorable impression possible. You may be frustrated and tempted to tell key people off, but don't. It's shortsighted, in spite of the temporary personal satisfaction you may get. You have a lot to lose in terms of favorable references from your company, the goodwill of your associates, and the word getting around outside the company—which can only hurt your job search.

WHEN AN EXECUTIVE RECRUITER KNOCKS ON THE DOOR

Executive recruiters are always looking for good candidates to fill their positions. A common technique they use to find them is for the recruiter to phone people who hold similar positions in other companies, to tap into their network, but it's also a way for the recruiter to see whether the person being called is interested.

When you're called out of the blue, if you can't talk privately or are caught by surprise, ask to call the recruiter back in private. Ask that a job description be mailed to your home and say that you'd like to think of suitable candidates and call the recruiter back. If you don't know him, ask for references to protect yourself or anyone you might recommend. It's flattering to be contacted by a recruiter, but be on guard.

Developing rapport with recruiters can be beneficial in the long run, but be careful. If you're comfortable with him and his reputation, try to be helpful, and try to refer appropriate candidates if the job isn't a possibility for you. Keep a list of these recruiters in your Rolodex because you can then contact them when you are job searching and remind them of when they spoke to you and why.

Being approached by another company can indicate more serious interest than being approached by a recruiter. Here again, consider how attractive the opportunity sounds. Evaluate the job as you would any other. If you're in good standing in a successful company, be doubly cautious in researching any such possibility because if your interest is even suspected, you could get fired.

Let's now look at alternative careers.

CHAPTER 16

ALTERNATIVE CAREERS

Many job hunters consider changing careers, particularly as they approach midlife. Actually, the vast majority of those who consider doing it decide against it, after they've done the research. Often people make such a change and then find themselves locked in, and, although they enjoy their new role, it doesn't meet their expectations. For some, however, a change can be the highlight of their career—in providing job satisfaction as well as more money.

Here are some of the most frequently chosen alternative careers:

- Consulting
- Temping
- Holding several part-time jobs
- Starting a new business
- Buying an existing business
- Transferring to another functional area in the company
- Working for a nonprofit organization or an activity, such as a trade association

Some general guidelines are given in this chapter for each of these alternatives. These general observations merely provide a starting point for more intense research on any alternative that you're attracted to.

MOTIVATION

Most people who consider alternative careers are attracted to them because of the possibility of reducing exposure to company politics, of avoiding some of the restrictions they work under in a company, and of getting more job satisfaction and control over their lives:

* "It's your baby" is a major consideration for many. Unfortunately it's still your baby when things go wrong.

* Some people want to be able to continue the activity after normal retirement age, people already well along in their careers.

* A principal enticement is often envy of people who are successful and on their own.

If you're strongly inclined to change careers, you ought to explore it. Otherwise you may look back on this as a lost opportunity for the rest of your life. If you choose to research one or more of the options, you must do it very carefully and thoroughly, as you'll see.

In the early stages of seeing people, keep an open mind on the various options that come up. As your search progresses, things such as consulting that you weren't attracted to originally may seem worth exploring.

REALITIES

In many of these alternatives, you're on your own in an entrepreneurial role. You no longer get a salary and fringe benefits in most of the options.

* Assess yourself and test your thinking with several friends: "Do you have the skills and temperament required to be successful in your contemplated option?"

* Most who choose an alternative career settle for less success and lower compensation than they had anticipated, but it still may be a good choice.

- It's important to assess your chances of success realistically, including how happy you'll really be (day in and day out).

- Make a very conservative cash projection. When people err on such projections, they're almost always overly optimistic. Get several people you trust to be realistic critics. Be sure to ask yourself and think carefully about the answer: What is the worst thing that can happen?

- In these entrepreneurial types of activities, your income usually takes a much longer time than you expected to reach an acceptable level.

- Realistically test with several friends, "What are the worst things that could happen and their likelihood?

- Ask yourself, "Why didn't you try to make this change sooner?" The people who are most successful in changing usually do it early in their careers, when they realize that they're never going to be happy working for somebody else.

- What's your exit plan, if the new career fails?

RESEARCH

When people look back at a failed alternative career, most recognize they didn't do enough research and weren't realistic enough in assessing the requirements for a successful change:

- Start by reviewing and updating the self-assessment exercises pages relative to the alternative career option you're thinking of.

- Your principal tools in this research are networking and informational interviews with people who are knowledgeable about the alternative you're thinking about. Reading several books on your chosen alternative can give you added insight, as can chat rooms on the Internet.

- Most job hunters, even though they've been successful and smart, bring a narrower view than they realize to a decision on a job alternative.

- *It's most important that you* talk to some people who actually made or tried to make the change you're contemplating. People who tried and failed are particularly useful because they probably have a more realistic view of the problems you'll be facing.

RESOURCES AND SERVICES

A lot of material has been written about many of these alternatives. The Internet is a particularly good source if you can find the right site for the particular alternative you're interested in. These sites often give merely an overview, but it's a start. Chat rooms can be a good source. In addition:

- Your best resource is networking with people who have made the change you're contemplating.

- Another very useful source is experienced retired executives of the Service Corps of Retired Executives (SCORE). Check out its Web site, www. score.org. This organization provides retired businesspeople as consultants at no charge. Many are very capable and will devote a lot of time to helping you.

- The Small Business Administration (SBA) provides considerable help to small businesses. Check www.government_guide.com or keyword: small business administration.

- A final, very useful source, once you have made a commitment to an alternative role, is a paid consultant for your specific needs, such as on marketing or technical issues.

Let's now look at some of the principal considerations in selecting one of the most common alternative careers: consulting.

CONSULTING

This career option is very attractive to many because it is easy to get into, it can be started very quickly, and it usually requires little capital. Sometimes people being laid off are asked to consult for their former company, which gives them a start. Most, however, have to start from scratch. Start by doing some self-assessment: What are your most marketable skills and experiences? You've already worked through this same self-assessment process, but now you should review the results relative to your considering consulting. Particularly useful is talking to other consultants, preferably in competing fields, who can give you tips on how best to position yourself, what kinds of companies offer the best potential, what are the principal problems you're likely to encounter, and how to cope with them. Most consultants take three to five years to achieve an income comparable to their last salary and fringe benefits. In your research, talk to some people who tried consulting and didn't stick with it. Most quit because they couldn't generate acceptable income, but often there are other reasons too.

Marketing

Spend at least a third of your time marketing, probably for the first three to five years, or until you get a steady enough stream of assignments to generate acceptable income. It's easy to avoid spending this much time on marketing, so keep track daily of the time you spend on it. If you're not generating the income, you should be spending one-third of your time marketing. You may be faced with having to skimp on marketing in order to do a first-class job on the assignments you have.

Your best potential for more work is to expand your current assignment. First of all, you have to do a really good job at it. Be alert to needs that you see and to ways your assignment could be expanded. Your next best potential for work is from previous clients. It's easy to forget about them when you get busy on another job, but they're important—and relatively easy to keep in touch with.

One issue to consider is whether you give clients what they think they want or what you think they want. You're best off to tell clients clearly what you think would be best, explaining your reasons, but be willing to compromise to keep a client happy by giving them what they want.

A good source of leads and introductions is networking. Targeted letters can also be useful in getting an opportunity to discuss possibilities with a company. Review the chapters on networking and selling yourself because marketing for consulting is similar to marketing in a job search.

In marketing your services or in working on an assignment, identify the real decision maker. It probably isn't the person you're working for on the assignment but his or her boss. The decision maker is the most important person you have to please. Expect some jobs will be cut back, canceled, or deferred.

Review Chapters 4 through 6 to develop a good flyer for your marketing. Networking can be useful in developing a marketing plan to get your first assignments.

Pricing Your Services

Your best guidance on pricing is sounding out your network of other consultants. Potential clients will make clear what they're willing to pay for your services. Decide whether you'll shave fees to get business. Your decision depends on how busy you are and your judgment.

Probably the easiest clients to get when you start out are small and startup companies. Unfortunately, these companies are ones who are probably the least willing to pay your established fee. You may even have difficulty collecting any fee. You may be offered a stock option in lieu of cash, particularly by a startup. It's unlikely you'll be as fortunate as Max Ernst, who several decades ago took half his fee for a modest job in the stock of a company with 10 employees. Today the stock is worth 1000 times what it was when he received it, several million dollars. He still has second thoughts over not having accepted his total fee in stock.

Help

Consider joining a group of noncompeting consultants, for several reasons:

* You can share an office and its expenses.
* You can exchange leads for jobs: Your associates may turn up leads for your specialty, and you may do the same for them.
* The group gives you an entity you belong to and overcomes some of the loneliness of consulting.
* You'll meet periodically with the group, exchanging information and discussing mutual problems, such as marketing, pricing, and potential clients.
* An alternative is forming your own informal group with a couple of noncompeting consultants whom you meet with periodically for the same purpose.

You should also consider having your own consultant for particular help. Because marketing is so critical and probably a real weakness, look for somebody for a reasonable fee who'll help you develop a good discipline and skill in marketing yourself and using your time effectively. Mary Powell found such an individual when she was starting out. In about a year, her practice had grown to over six figures, a level rarely obtained after several years by most consultants starting out. Unfortunately, she learned other real drawbacks to consulting: It's a lonely activity, her specialty was narrow, and the work was less challenging than her previous senior management job. Furthermore, she felt that her specialization reduced her job mobility.

She was also frustrated by the frequent gutting of her recommendations and by being excluded from their implementation, which was what she really enjoyed in her former company.

TEMPING

Many of the original temping agencies were started by companies like Manpower providing people to work on short-term assignments for clerical and blue-collar jobs. Subsequently, some of these agencies expanded into providing help for such an activity as software engineering. In the last decade or so, some agencies have expanded to provide managers, key staff people, and professionals to companies needing temporary help.

It's relatively easy to get into the database of a temp agency, but it may not do you much good unless you have strong skills. It's often helpful to network to get an introduction to one or several agencies. Most agencies have a large pool of workers, but often less than 10 percent of those in the database get a significant assignment in a year.

Here are some ideas on how to get assignments and succeed in carrying them out:

- An interview with a temping agency is similar to a job interview. Make sure you're prepared, using the interview preparation and effectiveness guidelines in Chapters 11 and 12. Your goal is not only to get accepted for its database but to make such a favorable impression that you'll be considered as a strong candidate for one of its assignments.

- Be persistent and sensitive in actively and imaginatively following up with the agency for assignments.

- Getting your first significant assignment is key.

- It's important that you perform well on any assignment. Agencies will give the best assignments to those people whom they get the best feedback back on.

- As you're completing each assignment, try to get the company to make a favorable report on your performance to the agency. Be prepared to defuse any unfavorable report.

- Many temps dream of getting an assignment that leads to a permanent job with the company. It does happen, but much less often than you think. Unfortunately, many companies prefer using "permanent" temps rather than adding them to their payroll. Encourage an agency to give you assignments with companies most likely to hire temps full-time.

- Temping is suited for those at a stage of their careers in which they're willing to have part-time work, but it may be less satisfactory for most who are trying to earn their prior compensation.

- Some agencies provide fringe benefits to their workers.

- Use your network to identify the agencies that are likely to be best for you, and continue to upgrade your list until you achieve an acceptable level of income.

- A useful book on temping is *Executive Temping: A Guide for Professionals*, by Saralee T. Woods (New York: J Wiley and Sons, 1998).

BUYING A BUSINESS

Buying an existing business seems attractive, but actually only a small percentage of those who seriously consider it end up doing it successfully. It usually takes much longer to make an appropriate purchase than it does to conduct a job search. Most potential buyers focus on the two biggest initial problems: finding a suitable company that's affordable and arranging the financing, assuming they'll be able to operate the business successfully enough to achieve their financial goals. This assumption is sometimes naive and leads to disaster.

The first consideration in thinking of buying a business is to see whether or not it's really an option worth contemplating because, at the very least, it's usually a time-consuming option. Some of the key considerations for people trying to buy a business are as follows:

* *Are you willing to take a substantial financial risk?* For most established businesses, you'll probably have to put up a substantial part of your own assets. Lenders view this as their best insurance. You also need financial resources to carry you through the expected search phase, which can be up to two years to bring about a successful purchase. You'll also need the additional capital to bring about the changes you feel are necessary.

* *Do you have the substantial backing of your family, particularly your spouse, in the length of time, the long hours, your near total absorption, and the risk in this endeavor?*

* *Are you willing to make the personal commitment of the length of time necessary to find the business and bring about its purchase?* That's only the start. You're then faced with the extensive time required to take over and organize the business the way you want, particularly in the first two years, and generating the increased profits you're counting on to pay off your loan.

* *Have you done this before?* Several studies show the most likely people to be successful are those who have done it successfully before or have been division heads of a substantial entity of a company. A useful book is *Buying Your Own Business* by Russell Robb (Adams Media Corporation, 1995), which gives you a broader understanding of the kind of commitment you'll be making and a much broader explanation of the things you have to do well to make it a success.

* *Are you a sound decision maker?* An associate professor at the Harvard Business School, Walter Kummerle, has recently completed an in-depth study of 50 startups. In his article, "A Test for the Fainthearted" in the *Harvard Business Review* (Boston, MA, May 2002), he cited that an entrepreneur starting up a venture

was faced with about 150 key decisions before the business started. This happens frequently. Buying an existing business ordinarily requires almost as many. Will you be comfortable making so many decisions, often without the information you'd like? This new role can be a lot more demanding and risky than you were used to as a successful manager.

Let's look at some of the issues you'll have to deal with. Completing the purchase successfully is only the first. Many people think they can get the money to pay for a business by improving earnings, but they overestimate their ability to achieve this and underestimate the amount of work and skill required to do so. People see friends buy businesses and make them successful. The experience seems attractive, but these potential buyers often underestimate what it took in the way of hard work, skill, and luck. Buying a business successfully requires finding a suitable opportunity at a reasonable price that they're capable of running successfully. It has to be a good fit with the buyer's skills and expertise.

The search phase takes many months of in-depth screening of several opportunities to identify one or two that meet the buyer's key criteria. Then the buyer focuses on one business, getting the potential and problems assessed by an expert, the finances evaluated by an accountant, and the complex purchase and financing documents drawn up by a lawyer. These tasks are time-consuming and costly. Success depends on the right timing and some good luck. Many potential buyers have gone through this process and gotten into final negotiations, only to have someone overbid them at the last minute.

The next issue is deciding whether you have the skills and experience needed to oversee the company's operation to improve earnings enough to make the purchase successful. Do you have the temperament to bear ultimate responsibility for the numerous details that have to be dealt with as well as developing and successfully carrying out a strategic plan necessary for the company's success?

Will you be able to deal with an unsuccessful purchase? Sometimes a bad purchase is due to the buyer's being too optimistic or to bad luck or to poor timing. You may be hit with a bad economy, a competitor's new product, or even a new competitor. You may then be faced with having to put up substantial additional capital or be forced to sell at a great loss.

You have to have the drive, be innovative, be stable emotionally to oversee the company's operations, and realize that the demands of the business are always hanging over your head.

Early on, ask yourself why you are doing this now if you're well along in your career. A great many people become entrepreneurs pretty early in their careers. Often, they've worked for others and recognize that they are never going to be happy unless they have their own show. Those who become entrepreneurs considerably later in their career often find it's very different from what they expected.

Dave Weinstein had been a successful General Division Manager managing about 100 employees. After he purchased a company, he went to his office the first day hoping to start to learn the details of the business and to get to know his key people. He was charged up to start putting his stamp on the company. First off, he asked his secretary what was going on that he ought to know about. She replied, "The biggest problem is that the driver who delivers our merchandise to our warehouses has called in sick." Dave replied with the question, "Who takes his place?" She said, "Well, we usually have to scramble around to find somebody." The first week on the job, Dave drove the truck to the company's various warehouses. Although that wasn't what he expected to be doing, it was a surprisingly good introduction to learning some of the nitty-gritty of the company's operations.

Bill Farrand was another successful senior executive who bought a business. He knew that he had to expand his sales greatly to make the venture successful. He soon learned that his two long-time salespeople had close relationships with several accounts that represented most of the company's business. It was possible that he would lose the accounts if he replaced these employees, but he needed people in their roles who would be aggressive salespeople who could bring about the sales expansion needed to make the purchase successful. He decided to retain the salespeople, but his timetable for this badly needed increase was set back more than a year.

Before purchasing a business, it's important to assess the business operations carefully, usually with some good consulting help, to see whether the business looks as strong in the immediate future as it has in the past. Are there any skeletons in the closet? How real is the potential for expanding it and making it more profitable? Identify why the business is up for sale—not just the stated reasons but the real reasons. Evaluate the possibility of a successful business going sour. Businesses fail all the time, often because of circumstances beyond the company's control.

A consultant friend told me he had three owners who reported to him that each one's respective several million dollar stake in the company largely disappeared overnight when new competition came on the scene. Two of these men had long-term loans, and they had to take out second mortgages on their homes to keep their business afloat. Even this additional financing might not turn the tide. In fact, there was a good chance they'd lose the business altogether as well as their comfortable financial positions. So be realistic about the risk and the amount of additional capital needed to save what may be a shaky situation.

Get a strong, active working board of directors with good experience in different functional areas. Select board members carefully, get them to commit to spending substantial time providing advice and being readily accessible at least by phone.

If you can bring off a successful purchase, running your new business may be a wonderful career for you. Tom Donovan started out working for others and quickly realized that he was an unhappy caged lion. He started two businesses, each with a suitable partner, but, after a few years, decided he wanted to step up to a bigger situation. Because of his industry knowledge in a rapidly growing new field, he was able to buy a struggling old-style company and modernize it with considerably improved profits. He built his new company in this very competitive business into one of the leaders in a large region. After several decades, he sold it very successfully to a large national company with several comparable facilities nationwide. A principal reason the national company made the purchase was buying his expertise to upgrade their own operations with the state-of-the-art processing equipment and the innovative distribution systems he had developed.

STARTING A BUSINESS

For some people, starting a business makes a lot of sense because they have good expertise and very strong motivation. However, if you expect compensation comparable to what you could earn in a regular job, you may be deluding yourself, at least initially. If you're successful and meet your financial expectations within a reasonable time, starting a business can be very satisfying. It's usually more work than you think, though it often can be started with much less financial risk than buying an existing business. Many aspects of the process are like buying a business, but they're more complex, because you have to deal with getting the business set up as a legal entity and managing all the necessary legal and financial aspects of getting the business officially established. Then you must set up the many activities necessary to run the business:

- Review the material in the previous section, "Buying a Business," because many of the characteristics of starting a new business are very similar to those of buying a business.

- You must first do the research on the potential businesses you're interested in and determine realistically the market potential of the one that offers the particular products or services you're considering.

- You have to find a location, equip the facilities, hire the employees, and develop your operating and accounting systems.

- At the same time you have to build up the business starting from nothing, covering your expenses including your personal compensation and generating enough profit to meet your obligations to lenders or investors.

- Have in-depth discussions through your network with people who can put you in touch with those who have started a business successfully as well as those who failed to bring it off.

- In the earliest stages, get some general information from the Internet and tips from such sources as governmentguide.com.

- Get a SCORE consultant to help you.

- Get a strong but small board of directors with diverse backgrounds who are experienced in startups and are willing to make a substantial time commitment to help, and who have backgrounds to fill in where your background is deficient.

MAKING A TRANSFER TO ANOTHER FUNCTION IN YOUR COMPANY

Occasionally, someone well along in a career may consider changing to a job in a different functional area in the company, for example, from Operations to Sales. To switch areas successfully, a person must be well thought of in the company and have particular skills that apply in the other activity. It's very unlikely that an experienced person can make a career change by joining another company, without doing so at a lower level than their previous job.

Start off by reviewing carefully the self-assessment exercises "Job Priorities," page 25, and "Who Are You?," page 27. If transferring makes sense, approach a key person you have a good relationship with in the functional area you want to transfer into. Tell this person of your interest. Prepare for this meeting as you would for a job interview. Transfers don't happen overnight, so be patient.

Fred Macomber was the Chief Engineer of a company that had about half of its business in custom-designed equipment. Over the years, Fred became more and more an administrator, which took him away from his great love of solving complex engineering problems. The company had a major sales engineering function, which backed up the sales force by developing products designed to meet special customer needs. When this Chief Sales Engineer role opened up, Fred was a natural choice for it, leading to his spending the rest of his career in this satisfying activity. Sometimes such a move means a cut in salary and authority, but for some such a sidewise move is a good choice.

WORKING FOR A NONPROFIT OR A TRADE ASSOCIATION

Some people want out of the corporate rat race. Working for a nonprofit organization may offer such an opportunity, frequently, but not always in a less pressured atmosphere. Sometimes it also offers a chance to work for a cause that you're particularly interested in.

A decade or more ago, many of the key people in nonprofits came from business backgrounds. It still happens, but less frequently today. Many nonprofits are looking for able people whose experience has been in their nonprofit field. A good example is in fund-raising, where the demands of today's sophisticated development activities require very special expertise.

When you change from a business to a nonprofit, you forfeit some degree of job mobility because it will be considerably harder to go back to another traditional job in a for-profit business if the nonprofit experience doesn't work out.

In nonprofits the board of directors often has more influence than it does in a business, overseeing closely the activities of key executives. With the often frequent turnover in directors, the key executives may find their positions in jeopardy because a new director wants to bring in his own person, to leave his particular stamp on the organization.

Frank Montgomery was hired out of industry to be the Vice President of Finance of an important university. He did reasonably well for several years, until the board of directors hired a major consulting firm that recommended that his role be filled by somebody with extensive financial expertise in educational institutions. Frank was let go. Fortunately, he was hired shortly afterward as the CFO of another major university. When he retired 20 years later, he was the Executive Vice President of one of the largest universities in the country, the capstone of a very satisfying career.

The search for a job in the nonprofit sector is essentially the same as for one in a private-sector business.

CHAPTER 17

MAKING THE NEW JOB AND YOUR FUTURE A SUCCESS

TRANSITION

A Good Start

You've achieved your goal of landing a good position, but it's only your first hurdle. Maybe the new job is what you really looked for, or maybe it's just OK. At this point, because you've accepted the position, you've got to develop a positive attitude about it. Now your goal is to make a successful transition. At least you no longer have the trauma of being without a job. You're still facing a period with considerable tension, that of getting settled successfully in your new role.

If you had a long job search, you'd be smart to take a week off—perhaps two—to wind down from the stress of it. Have some fun, but also clear the deck and get emotionally prepared for the new job. For some time you have been focused on getting a new job, dealing with those pressures and activities to the exclusion of pretty much everything else. Then, in the last few weeks, you've had the additional pressure of making the final decision, which may have involved developing other options or choosing between several jobs. Now you must put all of this turmoil behind you and focus on the job ahead. Take a day or two to organize your knowledge of your new company, its problems, your particular role, what will probably be expected of you, and what you think your initial assignments will be.

Think about the introduction you've had to other jobs, particularly if they were at a new company. Were there some problems you didn't handle as well as you would have liked? Did you ever upset anyone early on? What do you wish you had done differently? Think also about former associates coming into the companies where you've worked and any mistakes they made. Think about what effect your appointment will have on the organization. Whatever legacy your predecessor left for you, your goal is to succeed in the new job and to do it as smoothly as possible.

A key to making a success of the job is the determination to succeed. When the major sports leagues have their annual drafts, the teams select players very carefully. The players who are picked in the early rounds look like they're going to be stars, but some of them don't make the grade. Some players who are picked late or not picked at all become stars. A key difference in their success is in their determination to succeed. Make success your top priority.

The day you come aboard (and sometimes before), an announcement will be made about your appointment. If possible, try to discreetly discuss this announcement with your prospective boss ahead of time, agreeing on a few things about you to include and a few to avoid.

Consider how your new job affects your family. Very likely, the job will mean greater pressures on you at first, until you settle in, because of the tension of wanting to make a good impression, longer hours, and unanticipated problems. The pressure should be less, however, than what you were under during your job search. Moving to a different location may be particularly difficult for your family. Whatever changes there are, balance your family's needs and the demands of your new job as best you can.

The New Company's Culture

Observing how people behave and interact in the new company will help you understand how the company operates and how you have to act. Is it sales oriented or internally oriented? Are interactions fairly loose and informal, or are they highly structured? Are the key people continually involved in meetings or largely working on their own or working in small groups? What's the style of communication in meetings? Does one person dominate, or does everybody get involved? How does this communication differ from what you're used to?

Keep a low profile in the first week or two, even though you may be expected to hit the deck running. Many people will form an opinion of you in a few weeks, and you'll be carefully watched for several months. Be particularly sensitive to how most of the people treat you so you can interact with them best. Three obvious things to be aware of:

+ Observe the dress code and follow it.

+ Observe the length of day that's generally worked. Arrive a half hour early and stay a half an hour late. Observe who's there outside of working hours and whether they're working.

+ Observe the lunch routine. See when people go, when they return, and who goes with whom. Try to mix with many different people, and avoid getting tagged with a group.

Your Relationship with Your Boss

Remember that your boss liked you when you were hired and that your success depends on successfully nurturing this relationship. It's been said that more people get discharged because they don't get along with their boss than they do for performance. The key to establishing a good working relationship is to satisfy the boss's needs.

What are the pressures on him or her? Your priority is to help your boss do what he or she feels needs to get done.

Observe your boss's hangups and be sensitive to them. Is your boss a stickler for detail? Is getting work done on time a priority? How does the boss like to be communicated with? Does the boss get upset easily? Over what kind of things? Learn to deal with the boss's quirks—we all have them. Finally, as you get established, remember wherever you go in the company, you're your boss's representative.

Soon after you start work, ask the boss to write down the priorities for your job, and show the boss your list of priorities so that the two of you can discuss and agree on them. Ask when you'll be evaluated and on what criteria. Ask what's going on in the organization that you need to know about. Have any promises and commitments been made on key decisions that affect you? Which key people should you meet? Are there any sacred cows in the organization you ought to know about?

Ask your boss to meet with you regularly so that you can learn how he or she likes things done. Explain how important it is to you to make the job a success. Emphasize that your first priority is to help him or her get done what he or she needs to get done. Work to show this isn't just a platitude—you really mean it. Explain that, early on, you may make one or two mistakes. Ask him or her to understand this and to point them out so you can avoid repeating them. Suggest that it would also be helpful that he or she be frank with you on any of your failings.

Ask to spend a few minutes in your regular meetings with him or her to discuss whether you're on track. Ordinarily such meetings will be held intermittently only during the first few months. When the period of regular meetings appear to be ending, tell him or her how helpful they've been and ask if he or she would consider continuing them. If you can continue these discussions, you'll get much more frequent assessment than your peers, who probably get only an annual review. Not only will you be more aware of what you need to do to satisfy your boss's needs but you'll also learn more about what's going on. If your performance has been strong, you should cement a good relationship with your boss. When you get criticism, make sure you make a real effort to correct what caused it.

You'll help your cause if you observe what's going on in the company. Is it curtailing its activities? Starting new activities? Get feedback from outside contacts who may be more knowledgeable about the "big picture" than you are.

Finally, as you get settled in, let key people (particularly your boss) know of your accomplishments. Make sure they're visible. Many people do good work but never get recognized for it because the most important people in the job hierarchy aren't aware of it.

Building Rapport with Other People

Meet with each of your key subordinates and peers in a get-to-know-each-other meeting. Make sure that they do most of the talking and that you listen carefully. Ask them what their current activities are and what their professional background is. What do they consider the main problems that affect their work? How can you help them deal with these problems? What are the things that aren't being done that should be? Are there any commitments that you should know about? Don't prejudge their needs. Briefly describe yourself and your background. Ask them if there are any particular things they'd like to know about you. Ask one or two appropriate people to tell you what happened to your predecessor. You'll be interpreting the answer to this question from a new perspective, being on board.

Be particularly sensitive to anybody who may feel he or she deserved your job. Pay particular attention to supporting that person. The touchiness of this situation may be accentuated by the particular attention that you're likely to get as a newcomer. Now that you're on board, be particularly sensitive to the fact that in the interviewing process you were given attention by some senior people at a level above that of your boss. If you develop too close a relationship with any of these senior people, it may be resented by others. Respect everybody, particularly your peers and your subordinates.

It's important to listen and move slowly. In your job search you have learned to be a better listener; now's the time to use this skill on the job. Don't say, "This is the way we did it at XYZ." Rather, say, "Have you tried this? Do you think this might work?"

GETTING STARTED

Be ready for surprises. You may have misunderstood things that were told to you in interviewing or some of your assumptions may have been wrong. Lots of issues were covered. Usually such misunderstandings aren't critical. It's best to accept them as is—you'll probably lose more than you stand to gain if you make an issue of any of them.

You must demonstrate you're a good choice:

- Try to get along with everybody.
- Work hard to cooperate with others.
- Show that you're a hard worker and produce useful results.
- Be prepared to do more with less help—that's the way things are these days.
- Settle in quickly, but defer important decisions until you understand the culture and the real needs.
- Do simple assignments well. Very soon, you'll be working on your program and bigger projects.
- Come in early and stay late.
- Be on the lookout for opportunities in which you can make a special contribution unobtrusively without stepping on the wrong people's toes. Also be ready to step in and deal with emergencies.
- Don't brown nose, but volunteer for additional assignments.

All areas of a company have their "inner circle." Those selected have a preferred role; they're involved in key meetings, are sought after for advice, and are given special assignments. Unobtrusively, cultivate rapport with your boss and the other members of his or her inner circle, but make sure you don't step on toes doing it.

Your Productivity

A job search is frustrating, so it's easy to look at it as an unproductive gap in your career. If you end up with a job with good long-term prospects and have developed proficiency in some of the skills outlined before, you haven't lost as much as you think. You became a more effective job hunter, which can make you more effective on the job. Many of the new techniques you've learned can be very useful on the job. Let's review the key ones that were described in Chapter 13, "Conducting an Effective Search," and Chapter 15, "Should You Make a Job Change? (If You Have a Choice)."

* Set daily goals and grade yourself on your performance on the previous day's goals. Also include a checklist of deficiencies to improve on similarly. Make this process more effective by going public, by e-mailing this report to a friend.

* Use the techniques of dialoguing and failure analysis to make better decisions and better preparations for meetings and projects.

* Become a more effective—not aggressive—politician so that you're more effective dealing with people.

* Analyze your use of time so that you free up more of it for discretionary use.

* Identify needs and convert them into "showcase" projects, thereby getting the favorable attention of key people.

* Observe the superstars, and when appropriate, try to learn from them.

- Give yourself simple rewards for good performance and penalties for poor performance.
- Improve your conduct in meetings by being better prepared, by analyzing your performance, and by developing a preparation checklist for future meetings.
- Become more effective in selling yourself when dealing with those you interact with.
- Invite criticism sometimes to get good feedback on your performance.
- Hire an informal consultant if you need help on technical issues or on improving your performance.
- Make sure that your motivation is high to avoid the possibility of becoming passive and thus ineffective.
- Late Friday or over each weekend, tally your past week's performance and set your goals for the next week:
  - What did you accomplish this week?
  - What could you have done better?
  - Were there any areas of conflict this past week? What did you do to resolve them?
  - What are next week's goals?
- In your performance evaluations, learn from any criticism you're given. Demonstrate that you really listened, and take corrective action.
- If there's appropriate training offered, take advantage of it.

Your Technical Skills

Work on developing competence on the technology connected with your job. Especially keep your skills up to date using computers, networks, the latest software, and the Internet as these are needed on your job. Don't become a "techie," but do develop a relationship with one or two people who can help you keep current. If you find that you have a deficiency that really affects your performance on any aspect of your job, consider hiring an informal consultant. You'll probably find that a couple of evening meetings and having the consultant available for troubleshooting occasionally on the phone for a modest fee can get you up to speed quickly. Don't be embarrassed about it. Others have done it and have found it useful. It can also be useful in improving your performance.

An executive hired such a consultant when he became the CEO of a high-tech company whose technology he was unfamiliar with. He then led this company into becoming one of the great Wall Street success stories of the 1980s. This consultant got him technically up to speed in a month or so with a few meetings and occasionally discussing issues on the phone.

You should also keep current on your industry and your function (such as finance) by reading the publications your counterparts read and attending appropriate trade association and other relevant meetings.

Cautions to Watch Out For

Most job hunters find that the transition to their new job goes quite well, but occasionally it doesn't. It's already been pointed out that a new job doesn't work out more often than people think. This situation is obviously very serious, and it's important that you don't compound the apparent mistake by making another. So if your job choice may be a bad mistake, proceed cautiously but deliberately. Start off by reviewing your work on the self-assessment exercises (Chapters 3 and 13) along with your appraisal of the problems you've encountered on the job. What are the adverse and unexpected issues that have come up? Develop a correction plan and work at it. Take several months before you act. Discuss the situation with one or two trusted friends.

Bear in mind that one frustrating year out of a 40-year career isn't catastrophic. All people have ups and downs in their careers, even those who are most successful. Also realize you can develop valuable skills to make you more effective in the future by hanging on in a tough situation and learning how to make the best of it.

If you do decide to leave, expect to start from scratch in putting together another job search. You'll find that some of the people who supported you most in your just-completed search won't help you again. Some people leave a new job after just a few months, however, and they find with a new, aggressive search a more suitable job.

If after careful consideration, you decide you want to leave, it's likely that your boss also feels that hiring you was a mistake. Also this black eye for him is something he wants to handle delicately, without compounding the mistake. Of course, he may react that he wants you to leave immediately, but he may accept your suggestion that you stay on as a consultant for several months and have a reasonable amount of time off for your new job search. This compromise may be the best way out of a bad situation for both of you.

Sometimes the momentum of your job search results in one or two companies' or recruiters' approaching you after you've accepted your new job. Be discreet because you don't want to develop a black mark on your current job in case none of these situations works out. If you get an offer that's a substantial improvement over your new job, go back to your self-assessment and verify that it is, in fact, an improvement. Here again, you should discuss this with one or two friends. Be sure you're not making an emotional judgment based on a few troublesome incidents that have come up on the new job, which you should expect anyway.

PLAN FOR THE FUTURE

Within a month or two of starting your job, set aside some time to develop a plan for the next five years. What are the specific experiences

238

and skills that you need to hold down your boss's job? Who's an expert you might network with to fill in any gaps? What kind of reading should you do? It may be useful to discuss this with several of your peers at other companies because they're undoubtedly contemplating the same issues. Are there courses or seminars to fill in deficiencies in your experience?

Break down your plan into goals you set for yourself, say, for the next quarter. Assess your quarterly goals the same way you assess your daily and weekly goals. At least once a year, review your long-range goals to see whether they're realistic. The failure-analysis tool is a good device for being realistic about your plan.

Shortly after you get on the job, assess your financial status as a result of your loss of income during your job search. It's important to get yourself back on your feet financially in case you have to face a long job search sometime in the future.

When you look back on your search, you'll realize the importance of the help you've gotten from various people. For the benefit of your future career, nurture your best contacts by keeping in touch with them. Also work to expand your network. Try to join the appropriate trade association for your role. Regularly attend its meetings. When there, mix with the group and exchange calling cards to broaden your acquaintances. Call the most useful members of your network at least twice a year, just to keep in touch and to exchange ideas that can be mutually helpful. Make this brief phoning part of your routine every week. Also, cultivate relationships with the headhunters you know. When asked for recommendations for candidates, make a real effort to be helpful, which can only improve their opinion of you and improve the chances of their contacting you if they see you as an attractive candidate for one of their searches.

Finally, in your plan, be alert for various situations that can adversely affect you:

- Your company does badly, particularly if the poor performance involves the function you're in.
- You get considerable criticism in an evaluation; make sure you respond to this criticism by taking corrective action.
- You miss one or two of the objectives that have been set for you in your evaluations.
- You are not as productive as you could be.
- If you're cut out of the loop you've been in or are dropped from discussions or meetings you've attended in in the past, you may be getting a warning. Develop a plan to get back in the loop's good graces.

CONCLUSION

Your search has been successful and has put you on a strong road for the future. You've been forced to examine your long-term goals and to find a job in line with them. Don't look at the time spent in the last months as a real loss if you have positioned yourself well for the future. Sure, some of your peers may have moved ahead, but many have just stood still.

You've also learned that you can control your career more than you realize and some ways to improve your control in the future. You've emerged a strong, more realistic, and more effective person. Sure, it hasn't been easy, but having gotten a good job is a great accomplishment and step forward to a good future.

Good luck, and good hunting!

FREE JOB-SEARCH TIPS!

I sincerely hope that *The Executive Job Search* has been valuable in your job hunt. If you've yet to find your next great adventure, I hope you'll soon land it. If you've landed a position, I wish you every success! And I also urge you to keep in contact with many of the people you've met. Also, think of what you've learned that can be helpful on your new job.

No matter what your situation, you've undoubtedly practiced various techniques to get yourself across to the right people. Perhaps these techniques were unique twists on what you read in my book. You may have gotten great ideas from others. Or maybe you just learned a few useful things by trial and error.

SHARE YOUR TIPS!
E-mail them to me. I'll share additional tips with you.

YOU DON'T HAVE ANY TIPS?
E-mail me anyway and I'll also share these additional tips with you.

Whether you've landed a position or not, I'd like to try and help you. Some advice will be my own, others will be from others.

Sincerely,

Orrin Wood

Orrin@OrrinWood.com

INDEX

A

Accepting offers, 191
Accomplishments, 56–66
  description of, 135–136
  PARs, 61–66
  presenting, 60–61
  recognizing major, 57–60
  remembering, 56
  on resume, 78
  visibility of, in new job, 233
Advertisements:
  answering, 124–127
  jobs resulting from, 88
  resumes as, 68
  screening of responses to, 124–125
  writing job description from, 51
Advice, blind acceptance of, 16
Age factor, 8–10, 153
Alternative careers, 211–227
  age factor in, 9–10
  analysis of, 35–41
  buying a business, 219–224
  consulting, 215–218
  identification of, 35–36
  information resources on, 214
  motivation for choosing, 212
  nonprofit/trade associations, 226–227
  prioritizing, 38–41
  realities of, 212–213
  researching, 36–41, 213–214
  starting a business, 224–225
  temping, 218–219
  transferring in same company, 225–226
Alternative job analysis, 41–44, 190,
    192–193
Appearance, 8
  for interviews, 160
  of resume, 80–83
Appointments, number of, 163–164

Attitude, 1, 3, 7, 14
Attractiveness to employers
  (*see* Accomplishments)

B

Banks (as secondary recruiters), 129
Beginning a new job, 234–237
Benefits:
  negotiating, 188–190
  severance, 11–12, 189
The Benefits of Being Laid Off (Priscilla
    H. Claman), 12
Best Resumes for $100,000 + Jobs
    (Wendy S. Enelow), 65, 80
Best-worst decisions, 171
Blind prospecting, 111–119
  broadcast letters, 116–118
  jobs resulting from, 88
  methods of, 112–113
  PARs in, 66
  preparation for, 112, 118–119
  record keeping with, 119
  target letter mailings, 113, 114
  by telephone, 113–116
Board of directors:
  of nonprofits, 226–227
  for your own business, 223, 225
Boss:
  understanding feelings of, 200–202
  working relationship with, 231–233
Broadcast letters, 113, 116–118
Buddy system, 174
Businesses:
  buying, 219–224
  starting, 224–225
BusinessWeek, 203
Buying a business, 219–224
Buying Your Own Business (Russell
    Robb), 220

C

Career Initiatives Center (CIC), 2
Career Strategies, Inc., 12
Careers:
    choice of, 23–24
    phases of, 21–23
    (*See also* Alternative careers)
Challenger, James E., 164
The Challenger Guide (James E.
    Challenger), 164
Changes in work world, 10–11
Changing jobs, deciding about, 195–209
    another job in same company, 206–207
    and executive recruiters, 209
    how to leave company, 207–208
    myths about changing, 196–197
    reasons for frustration, 197–198
    and self-improvement program,
    198–206
Children, effect of job search on, 17–18
Chronological resumes, 68–71
Churchill, Winston, 6
CIC (Career Initiatives Center), 2
Claman, Priscilla H., 12
Closing (interviews), 154–156
College placement offices, 128
Communication skills, 131–132
Company culture, 231
Company research, 142–143, 185–186
Comparing offers, 190, 192–193
Compensation negotiation, 187–190
Consultant(s):
    for alternative career needs, 214
    working as a, 215–218
Contacts:
    continuing relationships with,
    106–107
    enlarging list of, 90–95
    getting interviews with, 95–99
    keeping in touch with, after employ-
    ment, 239
    unprofessional conduct with, 15–16
    (*See also* Referrals)
Contracts, employment, 189
Controversial subjects (in interviews),
    138

"Coping with Loss" (Robert B. Garber),
    2–3
Counseling, 18–19
    fees for, 19
    as severance benefit, 12
Counteroffers, 187
Cover letters:
    job requirement references in,
    124–126
    PARs in, 65
Criticism:
    of former employer, 14
    from networking interviewers, 105–106
    of resume, 81–82

D

Dates (on resume), 79
DBM, 88, 123
Decision process, 23–24
Demeanor, 133–135
Dialoguing, 169–171
The Directory of Executive Recruiters
    (William J. Morin), 26
Dragging campaign, checklist for,
    175–181
Dress code, 231

E

Education (on resume), 79
Efficiency, 19–20
Elevator drill, 94
Emotions:
    with job loss, 2–4
    in job search, 166–167
Employer's perspective, 45–53
    problems of employer, 45–51
    recruiting difficulties, 47–53
Employment contracts, 189
Enelow, Wendy S., 65, 80
Environment, job, 29–31
Exec-U-Net, 124, 174
Executive recruiters, 122–123, 209
Executive Temping (Saralee T. Woods),
    219
Executives, identification of (blind
    prospecting), 18
Exercise, 7, 168

Expenses:
  of job search, 17, 168
  relocation, 189

F

Failure analysis, 170
Failure of new job, 26, 183–184
Family:
  effect of new job on, 230–231
  and job loss, 17–18
Fees:
  counseling, 19
  of executive recruiters, 122
Final job candidates, criteria for, 48–49
Finances:
  for buying a business, 220
  contingency plans for, 16–17
Finance.yahoo.com, 119, 142–143
Financial aspects of job, 30
Five-year plan (for new job), 238–239
Formal organization, 200
Friends:
  as advisors, 6, 7, 174
  as contacts, 91
Fringe benefits, 188–189
Frustration, 197–199
Functional area changes, 25, 206–207,
    225–226
Functional resumes, 68, 69, 73–75

G

Garber, Robert B., 2
Gatekeepers, 95, 97–98
Globalization, 10
Goals:
  grading, 169, 201
  multiple mentions of, 172–173
  for number of interviews, 2, 163–164
  realistic, 7, 168
  in self-improvement program, 201, 203
  setting, 169
  (*See also* Job goals)
Grading (of goals), 169, 201
Granovetter, Mark, 89

H

Hair, 8
Harvard Business School alumni, 197

Headhunters, 239
Help:
  in consulting careers, 217–218
  job search, 174–175
Hidden agendas (of interviewers), 139
Hidden issues, 153
Hidden job market, 87
  blind prospecting for, 111–119
  networking to identify, 87–110
Hiring Managers:
  compensation negotiation with, 187
  job portrayal by, 156
  questions asked by, 145–146
  questions to ask, 147
Hoovers.com, 119, 143
Human Resources, interview questions
    by, 146–147

I

Impressions:
  postinterview improvement of, 157,
    160
  recognizing factors in, 48
Informal organization, 200
Information:
  on alternative careers, 214
  job/company, 185–186
Insurance (as severance benefit), 12
Internet:
  for alternative career research, 214
  job search help from, 174
  job search results from, 88
  recruitment via, 123–124
Internet resumes, 68, 69, 76–77
Interviewers:
  objectives of, 150
  observing traits/behavior of, 152
  researching, 143–144
Interviews, 141–162
  closing of, 154–156
  experimenting in, 136
  goal number of, 2, 163–164
  introduction phase of, 150–151
  listening skills for, 148
  networking, 99–101
  objectives in, 150
  obtaining, with contacts, 95–99

Interviews *(continued)*
  with other people in company, 156
  PARs in, 65
  postinterview activities, 157–160
  practice, 148
  preparing for, 141–148
  and references, 144–145
  research preparation for, 142–144
  selling yourself in, 133–140
  with temp agencies, 218
  tips for, 160, 162
  tough questions in, 145–147
  via Internet, 124
  from visible market applications,
    129–130
  work experience phase of, 151–154
Introduction phase (job interviews),
    150–151
Introductions:
  to executive recruiters, 123
  to referrals, 103–104
Invitation to criticism technique, 105–106

J

Job descriptions:
  by executive recruiters, 122
  writing, for job being sought, 51–53
Job fairs, 127–128
Job goals, 21–44
  alternative career analysis, 35–41
  alternative job analysis, 41–44
  in different career phases, 21–23
  financial, 30
  job objective in, 24
  lifestyle, 30, 31–32
  in new job, 238–239
  in normal job search process, 23–24
  prioritizing, 24–35
  and responsibilities/environment of
    job, 29–30
  and self-assessment, 26–29
  summary of, 31, 34–35
Job markets, 87
  hidden, 87–119
  visible, 87, 121–130
Job requirements, interview questions
    about, 146

Job search, 163–181
  avoiding pitfalls in, 14–17
  counseling help for, 18–19
  efficiency in, 19–20
  evaluation checklist for, 175–181
  family concerns with, 17–18
  and getting information on jobs,
    185–186
  getting started with, 163–168
  help with, 174–175
  improving productivity in, 169–173
  mental outlook for, 14
  for nonprofit work, 227
  personal habits for, 168–169
  preparation for, 13–20
  record keeping for, 20
  strategies for, 6–8
  while still employed, 207–208

K

Kummerle, Walter, 220–221

L

Lateral moves, 206–207, 225–226
Leaving:
  a company, 207–208
  a new job, 238
Legal actions, 12
Length:
  of resume, 79
  of work day, 231
Letters:
  for approaching referrals, 96
  broadcast, 113, 116–119
  cover, 65, 124–126
  target, 112–114, 119
  thank-you, 107, 157, 160, 191
  two-column, 125, 126
  upon-further-reflection, 157, 161
Lifestyle, priorities for, 30, 32–33
Listening skills, 148, 234
Lunch routine, 231

M

Market niches, 92
Marketing (of consulting services),
    215–216
Meeting performance, 204–205

Mental outlook (*see* Attitude)
Mistakes in job searches, 14–17
Momentum, maintaining, 167
Morin, William J., 26
Motivation:
    for alternative careers, 212
    improving, 205
Moving expenses, 189
Multiple mentions, 172–173
Myths about changing jobs, 196–197

N

National Ad Search Weekly, 124
Nationaladsearch.com, 51
Negative attitudes, 3, 7
Negotiation:
    compensation, 187–190
    stalling offer with, 184–185
Networking, 87–110
    after employment, 239
    analyzing network interview results,
        108
    building rapport, 100–101
    candid criticism from, 105–106
    for consulting careers, 216
    developing continuing relationships,
        106–107
    enlarging contacts list, 90–95
    finding information on referrals, 103
    getting networking interviews, 95–99
    and giving in return, 104–105
    for hidden job possibilities, 101–102
    at job fairs, 128
    jobs resulting from, 88
    personal introductions to referrals,
        103–104
    preparing for interviews, 99–100
    referrals from, 102–103
    success of, 88
    telephone interviews, 108–110
    12-step program for, 89
Networking resumes, 68, 72
New job, 229–240
    cautions in, 237–238
    failure of, 26, 183–184
    getting started in, 234–238
    planning for future in, 238–240

in same company, 206–207
    transition to, 229–234
New York Times, 124
Newspapers, 124
Next step approach, 173
Non-compete provisions, 190
Nonprofit associations, 226–227

O

Objectives:
    of blind prospecting, 112
    in interviews, 152
    in job interviews, 150
    of networking, 88
    on resume, 24, 78
Offers, 183–193
    accepting, 191
    comparing, 190, 192–193
    compensation negotiation, 187–190
    getting more job/company
        information, 185–186
    negotiation time with, 184–185
    using offer to get others, 186–187
Organization, formal vs. informal, 200
Outplacement services, 12, 18–19

P

PARs (problem-action-result) formula,
        61–66
    in blind prospecting, 66
    developing, 62–65
    expanded, 66
    in job interviews, 141, 151
    in networking interviews, 101
    relevance of, 64, 65
    in selling yourself, 135
    using, 65–66
    wording of, 61
Part-time jobs, 167–168
Patterns, work, 203–204
Performance, improving, 198–206
Personal characteristics:
    evaluation of, 49–51
    and executive recruitment, 129
    needed when buying a business,
        221–222

Personal characteristics *(continued)*
  selecting accomplishments to
    highlight, 59–60
Personal life, improving, 206
Perspective, job search, 1–12
  age factor, 8–10
  changing work environment, 10–11
  coping with job loss, 2–4
  focus on positive, 4–5
  and severance benefits, 11–12
  strategies for job search, 6–8
Persuasion, 131
Pitfalls in job searches, 14–17
Politics, playing, 198–200
Positive attitude, 1, 3, 14
Practice:
  interviews, 148
  on mediocre contacts, 7, 93
Preparation, 2
  for blind prospecting, 112, 118–119
  for interviews, 141–148
  for job search, 13–20
  of resume, 80–81
Presentation of self (*see* Accomplishments)
Pricing of consulting services, 216–217
Priorities, job, 24–35
  financial, 30
  lifestyle, 30, 32–33
  in new job, 232
  in responsibilities/environment of job,
    29–30
  and self-assessment, 26–29
  summary of, 31, 34–35
Private companies, researching, 143
Problem-action-result formula (*see*
  PARs)
Problems, potential employers', 45–47
Procrastination, 172–173
Productivity (in new job), 235–236
Promises, counting on, 15, 166–167
Prospective job:
  concept of, 47
  resumes reflecting, 85
  writing job description for, 51–53
Public companies, researching, 142–143

Q
Questions:
  inappropriate, 162
  preparing for tough, 145–147
  and Rule of Four, 185
  techniques for answering, 136–138

R
Rapport, building:
  in networking interviews, 100–101
  in new job, 233–234
Recessions, leaving job during, 208
Reciprocity (in networking), 104–105
Recognizing major accomplishments,
  57–60
Record keeping, 20
  for blind prospecting, 119
  during job search, 168
  for job search expenses, 17
Recruiters:
  executive, 122–123, 209
  interview questions by, 146–147
  questions asked by, 145
  secondary, 129
Recruiting, 47–53
  developing job description, 51–53
  falloff in, 165
  Internet, 123–124
  personal characteristics evaluation in,
    49–51
  technical abilities evaluation in, 49
References, 144–145
  from company you're leaving, 12
  resume mention of, 84
Referrals, 88
  asking for, 102–103
  getting information on, 103
  letter for approaching, 96
  from networking, 102–103
  personal introductions to, 103–104
  telephone interviews with, 108–110
  (*See also* Contacts)
Rejection, 7, 139–140
Relocation expenses, 189
Remembering accomplishments, 56–57

Research:
    of alternative careers, 36–38, 213–214
    of blind prospecting companies, 119
    of companies, 142–143
    of interviewers, 143–144
    of potential business start–up,
        224–225
Responsibilities of job, 29–30
Resumes, 67–86
    chronological, 68–71
    features of, 69–79
    functional, 68, 69, 73–75
    Internet, 68, 69, 76–77
    major problems with, 84–86
    and narrow concept of job, 47
    networking, 68, 72
    PARs in, 65
    preparation of, 80–81
    reviews/criticisms of, 81–82
    scannable, 69
    types of, 68–79
    writing tips for, 80
Rewards, 7
Robb, Russell, 220
Rule of Four, 185
Ruth, Babe, 138

S
Salary:
    negotiating, 187–188
    questions about, 102, 145–146, 154
SBA (Small Business Association), 214
Scannable resumes, 69, 123
Scheduling, 168
SCORE (*see* Service Corps of Retired
    Executives)
Screening:
    of ad responses, 124–125
    through telephone interviews, 162
Search firms/agencies, jobs resulting
    from, 88
SEC reports, 143
Secondary recruiters, 129
Self-assessment, 26–29, 198
Self-improvement program, 198–206
Self-motivation, 15

Selling yourself, 5–6, 131–140
    improving skills in, 131–135
    in new job, 236
    and rejection, 139–140
    techniques for, 133–139
Service Corps of Retired Executives
    (SCORE), 214, 225
Severance benefits, 11–12, 189
Showcase projects, 204
Skills:
    evaluation of, 49
    listening, 148
    needed when buying a business,
        221–224
    networking, 90
    selecting accomplishments to
        highlight, 57–60
    selling of, 135
    for selling yourself, 131–140
Small Business Association (SBA), 214
Socializing:
    visible, 174–175
    withdrawing vs., 94–95
Spouse, effect of job search on, 17
Stability of company, 31
Starting a business, 224–225
Strategies:
    for answering questions, 136–138
    job search, 6–8
Success:
    in job search, 1–2, 88, 165
    in new job, 230
Summary, resume, 78–79

T
Target letter mailings, 112–114, 119
Technical abilities:
    evaluation of, 49
    in new job, 236–237
Technical jargon (on resumes), 85
Technological innovation, 10
Telemarketing, 113, 116
Telephone interviews:
    for blind prospecting, 112, 113–116
    networking, 108–110
Temporary jobs, 167–168, 218–219

"A Test for the Fainthearted" (Walter Kummerle), 220–221
Tests, hiring, 162
Thank-you letters:
    after accepting offer, 191
    for job interviews, 157, 160
    networking, 107
Time:
    improving use of, 203
    for job search, 207
Time frames, decreasing, 173
Trade associations, 118–119, 175, 226–227, 239
Trade publications, 143
Transferring in same company, 25, 206–207, 225–226
Transition to new job, 229–234
12-step networking program, 89
Two-minute introduction, 142, 151

U
Underselling, 5–6
Unhappiness, reasons for, 198, 199
Upon-further-reflection letter, 157, 160, 161

V
Valueline.com, 119, 143
Venture capitalists, 129

Visible job markets, 87, 121–130
    advertisements, 124–127
    college placement offices, 128
    executive recruiters, 122–123
    Internet, 123–124
    interviews with sources in, 129–130
    job fairs, 127–128
    secondary recruiters, 129
Visualization, 138, 205
Voice mail, 95, 134–135

W
Wall Street Journal, 124, 127
Web sites, research, 143
Withdrawing, socializing vs., 94–95
Woods, Saralee T., 219
Work day, length of, 231
Work environment:
    changes in, 10–11
    for job search process, 164–165
Work experience phase (job interviews), 151–154
Work habits, 203–204
Workshops, 6, 174

Y
Yes-no decisions, 170

ABOUT THE AUTHOR

Orrin Wood runs a successful, Boston-based outplacement firm. He is a graduate of Harvard Business School and founder of the Harvard Business Association of Boston job counseling workshop, which has helped thousands of men and women find work at all stages of their careers. After 10 years in industry, he was Chief Financial Officer of S. S. Pierce Co. and Operating Treasurer of Massachusetts General Hospital. His *Your Hidden Assets—The Key to Executive Jobs* (Dow Jones-Irwin) was a Fortune Book Club selection and the principal book used by Harvard Business School alumni for over a decade.